Parents and Schools Together

Blueprint for Success with Urban Youth

Kelly Wachel

Foreword by Todd Whitaker

Published in partnership with the
National School Public Relations Association

ROWMAN & LITTLEFIELD EDUCATION
A division of
ROWMAN & LITTLEFIELD
Lanham • Boulder • New York • Toronto • Plymouth, UK

Published in partnership with the National School Public Relations Association

Published by Rowman & Littlefield Education
A division of Rowman & Littlefield
4501 Forbes Boulevard, Suite 200, Lanham, Maryland 20706
www.rowman.com

10 Thornbury Road, Plymouth PL6 7PP, United Kingdom

Copyright © 2014 by Kelly Wachel

All rights reserved. No part of this book may be reproduced in any form or by any electronic or mechanical means, including information storage and retrieval systems, without written permission from the publisher, except by a reviewer who may quote passages in a review.

British Library Cataloguing in Publication Information Available

Library of Congress Cataloging-in-Publication Data

Wachel, Kelly, 1979–
Parents and schools together : blueprint for success with urban youth / Kelly Wachel ; foreword by Todd Whitaker.
pages cm
"Published in partnership with the National School Public Relations Association."
Includes bibliographical references.
ISBN 978-1-4758-0851-3 (cloth : alk. paper) — ISBN 978-1-4758-0852-0 (pbk. : alk. paper) — ISBN 978-1-4758-0853-7 (electronic)
1. Urban youth—Education—United States. 2. Education, Urban—United States. 3. Education—Parent participation—United States. I. National School Public Relations Association. II. Title.
LC5141.W33 2014
370.9173'2—dc23
2013042446

∞™ The paper used in this publication meets the minimum requirements of American National Standard for Information Sciences Permanence of Paper for Printed Library Materials, ANSI/NISO Z39.48-1992.

Printed in the United States of America

For the Center School District family—past, present, and future.

And for my husband, Matt, and our kids, Maggie, Abe, and Lydia, all of whom would rather read books about fashion, cars, and dogs.

"What the best and wisest parent wants for his own child, that must the community want for all its children."

—John Dewey

Contents

Foreword		ix
Acknowledgments		xi
Preface		xiii
Introduction		1
1	Childhood	3
2	It's the People	9
3	What Makes a Good School District Great?	17
4	What Are Our Students Like Today?	23
5	Relationships and Responsibility	31
6	Having Quality Systems	35
7	The Academic Standards	41
8	Inclusion	63
9	Keeping Tension on the System	69
10	The Heart of a School	81
References		85

Foreword

When Kelly Wachel first sent me the idea for her book, I was fascinated. The idea of her book resonated with me both as a parent and as an educator. Kelly's book focuses on a challenge every school and district faces—making students college-and-career-ready. The project she and her team have been working on has had a tremendous impact in her school district and in the greater Kansas City area. Her goal in this project is to have other educational settings replicate the success her district has achieved.

After seeing the finished manuscript, I was encouraged by the message of parent and school responsibility in working together. It takes everyone—parents and schools—to raise successful students. It also takes knowing how to play the game—knowing what the rules are for parents, students, and schools, and also knowing the Common Core State Standards.

Because we are educators, we know the importance of parents reading with children daily, starting as soon as they are born. Most parents know about things like playing and pretending and laughing. However, there are other parents who do not have this skill set. It is essential that we guide those who do not have these natural instincts in developing the skills that will help their children and our schools continue to improve.

All parents reflect on whether they are doing the right things raising their children. Everyone does the best they know how. However, some people know how better than others. Every parent worries about whether they are doing what is needed to prepare their kids to be successful in school and in life. We wonder whether we read enough books, listen, talk, laugh, explore, and experience life with them. How do we give the correct direction and reassurance to all parents? How do we help all parents and every school think about the importance of raising all children to be successful students ready for college and a brave new world?

The value in Kelly's book lies in the guidelines she spells out for all parents and all students to master in order for the students to be advanced and ready for college. In the 1940s we focused on the G.I. Bill and getting veterans into college; in the 1950s we focused on dismantling the separate but equal doctrine with *Brown v. Board of Education*; in the 1960s we focused on getting all kids a high school diploma; in the 1970s and 1980s we focused on standards-based education, and then, in the 2000s, No Child Left Behind. The goal now is that every child be college-and-career-ready and prepared for a future we know nothing about.

The value of this book is also in the ideas Kelly shares regarding a specific plan for schools. She outlines how schools can take the Common Core State Standards that are essential for parents and students to know and put them into a medium that's easily understandable.

The parents who don't know what to do academically with their kids will be able to easily understand what to do after reading this book. And the schools that might not know how to communicate academic goals to parents and students will be able to easily comprehend what to do after reading this book.

With all the talk of *standards* and *is it right for our schools*, we need to be asking this question: *Is it right for what we want our children to look like in the future?* This book never forgets that kids are kids and that they need to be loved, nurtured, and pushed academically. Kids need to know how to be academically tough. Schools need to know how to be academically tough.

We can't have excuses anymore. There should be no excuses with all of the resources available today. It's everyone's responsibility to ensure that schools and parents can't come up with excuses for why their students aren't achieving. It's reassuring to know that there are schools and parents who are here to help.

I'm excited for Kelly's book as she shares her experience working with kids, parents, and schools. I am confident you will enjoy her reflections about people, leaders, responsibility, Common Core expectations, public relations projects, and pure nurturing of kids as much as I have.

Enjoy Kelly's book. Enjoy reading about her hopes for our schools and students. There is nothing we can do more to positively have an impact on the future than to nurture children in order to maximize their abilities. Good reading!

Todd Whitaker is professor of educational leadership at Indiana State University in Terre Haute, Indiana. He is a former teacher and principal and has written more than thirty books and has presented to hundreds of thousands of educators around the world.

Acknowledgments

First and biggest thanks to Tom Koerner, my publisher and editor at Rowman & Littlefield. Thank you, Tom, for convincing me that I had this book in me.

Thanks to Rich Bagin at the National School Public Relations Association (NSPRA) for joining the publishing effort. Thank you for seeing the importance of showing your members what urban education should be.

Thanks also to Todd Whitaker for encouraging me and for reassuring me that this book had potential. You have been a great source of support for me—in all stages of my life.

This book wouldn't have happened without Center School District—I owe much thanks to its students, parents, staff, and leaders. Special thanks also go to Bob Bartman, Dave Leone, Danelle Marsden, Angela Price, Beth Heide, Joe Gunderson, Sharon Ahuna, Sharon Nibbelink, Joyce Stokes, Linda Williams, Jason Steliga, Brad Sweeten, Sheryl Cochran, Tyler Shannon, Tamara Sandage, Aimee Alderman, Jim Hoelzel, Stacy King, Gary Pointer, Bruce Rehmer, Michele Ryan, Elizabeth Sweeten, Madison Noll, Brandon Roland, Sally Newell, Betty McKinzie, Cindy Noll, our Center Friends volunteers, and the board of education.

The design team at Design Ranch in Kansas City has been instrumental in helping Center School District with our brand and image. A big thank-you to Ingred Sidie, Frank Norton, and Claire Gude. You are talented and fun—and I am grateful for your willingness to work with us.

Thank you to my wonderful friends who supported me in writing this book: Sarah McKee, Dave and Suzanne Campbell, Carrie Trotter, Mike Fischer, Joel and Jill Ackerman, John and Cori Howard, Lindsey Trees, Sarah Hart, Katy Massa, and Laura Freitag. Please note, all of my friends are wonderful, and I thank you all, even if you weren't specifically mentioned here.

I also have to thank my brothers, Beau Harvey, Brock Harvey, and Lance Harvey, who helped me to learn what childhood was all about, and who never let me take myself too seriously.

Thanks to my mom, Peggy Vietti, for being the best example of a parent and a teacher.

And thanks to my husband and idea-bouncer, Matt Wachel, and our kids, Maggie, Abe, and Lydia. Maggie, Abe, and Lydia, you've taught me what it means to be a mom and how important it is to raise readers and pretenders.

Preface

There was a knife fight on the front steps of the high school. This is what I was thinking about when the newly appointed superintendent was talking about the job of the public information officer in his school district. He said, "Kelly, I have our public information officer job open. I need you to come do missionary work in public education. I need some help changing perceptions."

I was newly engaged, earning a private-sector salary in marketing and sales, and ready to breeze through a wedding, having kids, and making money. Then came an offer to work in a public school system (an urban public school system, no less) to help change the negative perception of its schools. Do *missionary* work. Don't misunderstand me. My heart longs to always help others, but my checkbook also longs for a solid private-sector paycheck. I was going to make money by working in the corporate world and climbing that ridiculous ladder.

However, as I was getting ready to marry a handsome kindergarten teacher, and as I was ready to get real about what my life was going to look like, it was natural that I said yes to the job of public information officer for Center School District in south Kansas City. That corporate ladder didn't make me feel like I was doing something that mattered. Maybe I could do something that mattered in a public school? *I like kids*, I thought, *and my mom is a teacher*. Anyone can work in a public school.

And that's where the perception-changing gig had to start. Not just anyone can work in a public school. I had to change my own perception of what it would mean to work in a public school—an *urban* public school. What it would mean to really work on behalf of public education and all kids.

In the 1950s through the early 1980s, Center School District in south Kansas City, Missouri, was a predominantly white, upper-middle class suburban community. Affluent neighborhoods were mixed with middle-income neighborhoods, while the north end of the community was more poverty stricken. Throughout the 1980s and early 1990s, though, the demographics of the community began to change. The schools went from that predominantly white, upper-middle class suburban demographic to what is today a school district of 75 percent African American, 20 percent Caucasian, and 5 percent Hispanic students. Seventy-five percent of these students qualify for free and reduced lunch.

In the district, which consisted of an early childhood center, four elementary schools, one middle school, one high school, and one alternative school, the 2,500-student population did a 180-degree turn in a matter of twenty years. It went from being a sought-after gem in south Kansas City to an urban demographic with provisional accreditation from the state of Missouri.

Provisional accreditation with a knife fight on the front steps of the high school. *Did you hear about the knife fight at Center High School? What's happening in those schools?* (I should mention here that the knife fight was merely a cut on a student's neck, and it didn't even involve a knife.) This is where the lore of Center School District's perception problems started. With that, and, of course, with the changing demographic from white to black.

So, with the story of a knife fight and the task to start changing perceptions, I started my job as public information officer with Center School District.

In thinking about changing perceptions, we had to think about working with parents and our schools on how to increase academic rigor so that our students would internally start busting the perceptions of low expectations and gradual failure. We had to shake the previous stamp of provisional accreditation and, together, learn how to get to the state's gold standard of "Distinction in Performance."

This task took seven years. After seven years of work—work that you will see hints of in this book—we received the designation of "Distinction in Performance" during the 2011–2012 school year. And on the cusp of a perfect 14 out of 14 on the annual performance review (APR) from the state in the fall of 2012, the leaders of our district started to bat around an idea based on the "seven keys to college readiness" from Montgomery County Public Schools in Rockville, Maryland. We knew that we needed to keep getting better, and the next step was to focus on college and career readiness for all of our students.

Montgomery County Public Schools compiled the seven indicators that are essential to creating college-ready students in its district. Based on their research, the seven criteria are as follows:

- Advanced Reading Grades K–2
- Advanced Reading Grades 3–8
- Advanced Math Grade 5
- Algebra I by Grade 8 (with a C or higher)
- Algebra II by Grade 11 (with a C or higher)
- 3 or better on AP Exam, 4 on IB (International Baccalaureate) Exam
- 24 on the ACT, 1650 on the SAT

We knew that we also needed to have some key indicators to help students and their families know what path to take and what standards to start aspiring to as they navigated their school careers.

Schools do a great job of teaching kids, but it has to go further. We knew we had to start helping students and parents by showing them the path needed to be college-and-career-ready when graduating from our district's high schools—and it had to start at birth. In a school district with a majority of poor, urban students, we knew that starting from birth would be imperative.

As a young mom myself, this topic and these ideas we were working with in our school district seemed to mesh completely with my own life. I was thinking about babies and toddlers and my oldest daughter getting ready to start kindergarten while I was also celebrating our school district's high school seniors walking across the stage at graduation. *There should be a guide for parents and students*, I thought. *We should be helping parents better understand their role in their children's education.*

We produced a project called *Made Smart* (found on our website at www.center.k12.mo.us) that we distributed in the fall of 2012 to the district's parents, students, and staff. This project became a success in that it helped us as a school and community focus on the next steps in preparing our students for success beyond high school. It also became a unifying force for our schools that started to seep into the broader Kansas City region.

I wanted to bottle this stuff up and sell it to everyone—parents, teachers, administrators, and students. But being short on that capability, I decided that a book would have to suffice.

My gift to you is this: a book that uses my experience in working with an urban school district from provisional accreditation to a perfect score on the annual state review and shows you how to pluck some of its tools for use in your own way. Whether a parent, a teacher, an administrator, or a student, the hope of this book is that it will help provide a sense of purpose in raising kids and students to be successful in life and in school.

Introduction

While reading this book, think about it as a guide to helping teachers, administrators, parents, and students work together on specific areas within the school experience to produce achieving students. A guide can have many instructions, but this book narrows the focus to a handful of high-impact strategies that administrators, teachers, and parents can use. Student learning is the goal of education, and there are ways described here to help enhance that goal.

To talk about student learning, today's schools need to start talking about the importance of teaching children from birth. No longer is it acceptable to allow early learning to be a function of a parent's economic means. The early childhood years must be influenced by the more rigorous goals of public education. Yes, these early years are about playing and pretending and having fun bonding with parents, siblings, and the world, but they are also about learning the essential ingredients to be successful in kindergarten and beyond.

Urban schools hear lots of excuses from all kinds of people—parents, teachers, leaders, and the community. *This is why it can't be done. It's not my job. It's the parent's fault.* Guess what? It can be done, it's everyone's job, and parents are definitely in need of some guidance when it comes to raising kids.

With that, this book is organized into ten chapters that stem from an approach to creating students and parents that work together with schools from birth to grade 12. The chapters cover such topics as creating a school district that is about people, literacy, and math, and creating a sense of inclusion. There is no silver bullet. That is a given. But we can identify specific elements that contribute to successful students and schools.

Here are some specific topics that this book will cover:

- Raising children from birth and how it affects kindergarten readiness
- Creating a school district that focuses on people

- Learning how to encourage people and spread the message of high expectations and academic rigor
- Helping students and their parents understand their role in education
- Developing relationships and responsibility within schools
- Having systems in place that exhibit professional, above-and-beyond care and attention
- Focusing on literacy and math (understand what Common Core State Standards parents and students should know—if you follow these standards, you are creating a path for advanced students)
- Taking those standards and advanced students and creating a sense of inclusion—building a community and school district that welcomes students, social services, and community business partners
- Keeping tension on the system and regularly communicating all these standards and expectations to students and their parents
- Thinking about childhood and how it translates into educating kids today

Raising kids and thinking about childhood and specific learning standards are the kinds of things that parents and schools think about every day. However, some parents (and even schools) need extra support and guidance in creating a framework for producing high-performing students. Parents need (and mostly want) their school to be the authority on helping them raise successful students, particularly economically disadvantaged families, many of whom did not have a proper school support system as kids.

One thing of note when reading this book: We all know that the school is the embodiment of the leaders, teachers, staff, students, parents, and community. I will use the term *school* in several instances in this book. Think about the term *school* as not being an inanimate object, but rather a living, breathing entity.

It's time to change our perspective. Let's think about schools and parents and their children being the only things that matter. Let's think about schools that are safe havens of fun and learning. And let's think about schools that become the measuring stick to which all other facets of society aspire to be like. With that comes the responsibility to think about education as the first priority as a parent—and then, as a school, the first priority becomes helping those parents raise that child to be smart, ready for school, and able to learn.

ONE
Childhood

Think about your childhood. Think about what your life was like growing up. Did you have two parents in your home? Did one or both of them work in a professional, consistent place of employment? Did you consider your family a middle-income or affluent household?

Most of the people working in a school district setting would classify themselves as coming from a middle-income household. Most of the school professional staff came from a model of what it looked like to have a successful child grow up, attend college, and get a good job.

These households generally had parents who read to their children, talked to their children, laughed with their children, played with their children, nurtured their children, loved their children—the children's needs were met quickly and often. This scenario was lived by most professional school employees during their childhood years. Again, think about it—wasn't it like your childhood?

Being born into a professional-type family in which one or both parents are college educated and have middle- to high-paying jobs is a scenario that is not mirrored everywhere. The world today does not reflect what most professional workers in the United States experienced in their childhoods.

It is becoming rarer, particularly among the economically disadvantaged, to have parents who raise kids to be readers, thinkers, workers, contributors, and overall responsible citizens. But it shouldn't be. Do not doubt that virtually every parent wants her child to be successful and healthy. Every parent wants what's best for her child. Success, however, is defined by each parent according to her life situation.

If you are a parent, remember the moment when you held your child in your arms for the first time. You looked down at that child, so fragile and so beautiful, and a tidal wave of love just poured over you. Inside of that tidal wave, you thought that you wanted only the very best this world has to offer this child. Remember how driven you were to protect that child from all the bad in the world, and remember how big your dreams were for your child at that moment. This is a unique and intimate experience for each parent. At the same time, it is a universal experience that parents all over the world share.

It is that premise—wanting to preserve that emotion of hope and dreams for children in spite of everything out there in the world, and knowing that all parents want what is best for their child—that schools and parents should think about when approaching student learning.

Regardless of whether parents know it, it is critical that they provide the appropriate stepping stones, starting at birth, to get their child kindergarten-ready, and, ultimately, to get to college-and-career-ready. As a school district, making sure each child in your care is ready for school is something you owe your district's parents because it is nothing less than what you want for your own children at home.

For parents and schools, a lot of thinking goes into academically preparing children for the future. However, the academic portion of parenting and schooling can come more easily if children receive strong nurturing and a literacy-rich environment from the beginning. Raising readers, critical thinkers, and responsible citizens starts with a sense of love and trust in their home. To be a kid is to feel free of burden. Playing, pretending, snuggling, laughing, failing, trying again, experimenting—these are all qualitative components of childhood. When these and other nurturing-type qualities are met, the quantitative components like singing the ABCs, rhyming, reading, counting, telling stories, and drawing can be inserted more effortlessly into a child's day.

Think about this research: A child who grows up in poverty has about 70 percent of the vocabulary of a working-class family and 45 percent of the vocabulary of a professional family. Children from professional families have heard 32 million more words than children who live in poverty. According to the research, kids from professional families have heard about 45 million words by the time they are four years old. Those living in poverty have been exposed to 13 million. This is known as the *30 million–word gap*.[1]

Not only do children of poverty have less exposure to vocabulary, but they also experience 500 affirmatives and 1,100 prohibitions each week. This means that these children hear twice as many negative than positive words each week.[2]

Being poor virtually automatically puts a family into the at-risk category. This means that a child is at risk because of any of the following criteria: households without English speakers, a large family that has four or more children, low parental education (both parents lack a high school degree), residential mobility (families who have changed residences more than once in twelve months), a single parent family, a teen mother, and/or nonemployed parents.[3]

In the wealthiest nation in the history of the planet, this gap in learning is a travesty. The way to fix it is to think about raising kids of poverty in a way that mirrors the experiences of a professional family. Schools have to figure out how to encapsulate the experience that a professional family provides their children and make it available to the families of poverty.

It is true that some would say that families don't want to be told how to raise their children. However, by building a good rapport between the school district and the community, you may find the opposite. Families are looking for guidance and help. It is the school district's duty to provide that guidance. For instance, maybe a parent doesn't know that she needs to look her daughter in the eye and sing nursery rhymes. Or maybe another parent doesn't know that he needs to hug his son and read every day with him. Families need to understand how to provide the basic needs of literacy and how to nurture their kids.

Who has the most direct access to parents and students who live in urban environments? The schools. Schools have to think about reaching these families differently than before. Schools need to think about how they reach out to families, put their arms around these families, and pull them into the confidences of raising successful children.

Most educators choose their occupation because they have the noble desire to help kids. It is a disservice to students if those educators and their schools are not engaging parents to be part of the solution in raising successful children. Together, educators and parents have to work at creating a school system that ensures success from the start.

When the shift from simply teaching students and communicating to parents about how their student did at school that day moves in the direction of being partners in raising kids together, teachers and administrators can be the leaders in providing proven advice to parents. The requirements of teaching today are more strenuous and involved than ever. There are teachers and leaders out there who understand this.

There has to be a tipping point at which these educators, who have the essential, inherent quality of sustained excellence, overpower the educators who do not. This has to be the qualification of educators—excellence in serving kids and their parents.

Do you know that parents who are more involved in their child's education tend to have higher-performing children? Of course you do. But is that notion harnessed enough? In some schools it is; in others it is not. It should be a priority to work with parents and students to teach them about the necessary steps at home to aid the efforts at school.

Parents and schools together, like the title suggests, is the mantra that has to be internalized for educating students. No longer can just parents or just schools raise and educate kids. It takes both. For most, it's too late when a child is three years old and she is unable to understand simple directions, follow a story, and draw freely on paper. The gap from age three to grade 3 is created even before the age of three.

There is current work happening around the age three to grade 3 gap—that is, the growth by some students from age three to grade 3 and the lack of growth by other students for the same time period. This early learning period in children's lives is critical for future success. Most educators know this. Most parents know this. But what has to happen now is the communication of this critical time period's essential skills to the parents who don't know this yet. Schools, and this nation, cannot afford to continue having third-grade students who cannot read.

If a student cannot read by third grade, he is unlikely to ever catch up to his peers ever in reading skill, fluency, vocabulary, or comprehension. Or, to put it another way, if a student cannot read by third grade, he is unlikely to ever have the skills necessary to compete in college or a professional career. There is also evidence that shows the reading ability of a child in third grade can predict his chance of becoming incarcerated.

Whoa, this is a lot of pressure on those primary teachers and their schools to have kids reading by third grade! But is it? Yes and no. And not when the fundamental literacy skills and foundation of support have already been internalized in students from birth.

If a baby comes home from the hospital after birth and is read to, talked to, cuddled, sung to, nurtured, attended to immediately, and provided for unrelentingly, then that baby will most likely grow into a toddler and then a kindergartner who has the foundation for reading, conversing, loving, rhyming, caring, and responding.

Think about where you learned to interact with and teach or parent a child. Most people might answer, *their own parents*. Children learn from their parents, and parents learn how to parent from their own childhood experience. If a parent never had the experience of reading, singing, talking, listening, learning, and nurturing while growing up, then that parent is unlikely to provide those same experiences for her own child.

The cycle has to be broken. Schools have to help parents break this cycle of not knowing. In this world that is so connected, there should be no reason for parents not to have key information about raising achieving students who are ready to learn in kindergarten.

When all kids arrive in kindergarten with the needed skills and knowledge to be ready to learn at high levels, all schools benefit from accelerated instruction. Whether it's from Parents As Teachers (an early learning program in some states that focuses on learning from birth to kindergarten), other moms and dads, a parenting book, or their own parental instincts, parents are going to learn and parent based on a template in their brains concocted from somewhere. It might as well be school-based people who have some expertise in student learning who help construct the framework for raising successful kids.

Chapter summary: Parents of children who live in urban communities where poverty and instability are the norm have to understand the simple joys and fundamental necessities of what it takes to raise a child who is ready for school. Schools have to help parents in this responsibility. If parents don't know what it takes to get a child prepared to learn at high levels, then someone has to teach them. Yes, childhood is about enjoying the simple pleasures of being a kid, but it's also about having the brain connected and ready to absorb reading skills, vocabulary, conversation, and imagination. Parents have to understand how to give love and nurturing along with the skills needed for learning. Parents have to learn how to give children a childhood.

NOTES

1. Betty Hart and Todd R. Risley, *Meaningful Differences in the Everyday Experience of Young American Children* (Baltimore: Paul H. Brookes, 1995).

2. Betty Hart and Todd R. Risley, "Meaningful Differences in the Everyday Experience of Young American Children," strategiesforchildren.org (August 2013), http://www.strategiesforchildren.org/eea/6research_summaries/05_MeaningfulDifferences.pdf (accessed August 15, 2013).

3. "National Center for Children in Poverty," nccp.org (August 2013), http://www.nccp.org/tools/risk/ (accessed August 15, 2013).

TWO
It's the People

Excellence. People. The previous chapter mentions the essential component of educator responsibility and parent responsibility and the component of people in schools who have to help get parents and students' mentality intertwined with student achievement. It's the people who have to create schools and homes full of achieving students.

The greatest companies (measured by profit and productivity) in the United States usually reference leadership and people as the key drivers of performance and success. This *people first* attitude seems to be the common denominator when looking at successful organizations. Schools are no different.

The leaders of a school district, starting with the superintendent, have to be the shining examples of excellence that they, in turn, will demand from their teachers and staff. This is not new information, but actually putting the highest-quality leaders in place seems to be a problem in some school districts. Why is that? Why is it so difficult sometimes to put the best people in leadership positions?

Some leaders are scared to leave the comfort of success in other schools, or they are too afraid to take the reins in an urban school. However, urban schools are not scary when they are nurtured and pushed by amazing people and leaders. The best leaders have to start leading the most challenging schools. Leaders and teachers cannot be afraid to take on failing schools. In fact, the best leaders and teachers should feel like the challenge of working in an urban school is a moral imperative. It takes a bit more to work in a school and community setting in which students may not be prepared for school and may not have the comforts afforded to them that other students have. It's these schools that need the best leaders and teachers.

Sometimes the compensation might not be equal to the quality and integrity required of the position, but in education, compensation can never truly reach the level it should for rewarding the most important job in America—the job of creating successful students. At the same time, school districts should want the people who have motivations other than money as their employees—the motivation should be to do good work on behalf of students and parents.

Up to a point, money is important. Money offers comfort, the ability to be secure, and the ability to make decisions more easily. But after the monetary threshold is met for most workers, there are reasons other than money that make people stay in education.

Maybe it's not all about money, though. Other times there simply isn't access to quality leaders, but this shouldn't be a hindrance to finding the right leaders. It just might take more patience. Finding the right leader is perhaps the most important task of a board of education and their community.

Schools and their boards of education have to understand the importance of hiring only the best leaders to work in schools. If it's all about the people, then the people have to be exceptional. It's not fair to the students when the people working in schools aren't the best. The leaders and the people of a school district are going to be the idea makers, visionaries, and workers. They have to be motivated to do the work that is required for teaching and learning at high levels. This work isn't for everyone, and schools shouldn't take just anyone.

Successful companies don't just hire anyone. They recruit and hire only the best fit for their organization. Schools also need to understand this process. While there does have to be flexibility in any organization in hiring a good fit for a position, that flexibility shouldn't be a settling of standards. Schools shouldn't *settle* on the people who are going to be teaching and learning with their students every day.

Schools should be motivated to find the best leaders and teachers because it's the people who will carry out the grand vision for a high-performing school district. This idea of motivation to do good work on behalf of students is needed because working with kids is the most important part of the whole deal. There are several fundamental motivations that leaders should have:

- the kids
- the teachers
- the other leaders of the district
- the parents
- the community
- themselves

Think about the *themselves* bullet point. Basically it means people should be motivated to do good work for their own sense of self. When people have a sense of purpose and a sense of freedom to do their job using creativity and their own specific skill sets, it produces an internal drive to do good work. But it's not only *for themselves* that leaders and their staff should do good work—it's also for the students, parents, their colleagues, and the community.

With each of these internal and external motivations, leaders and their staff have to be exceptional. They have to have exceptional integrity to make the right decisions. Whether leaders are beloved or liked or respected, one of the most important things that a leader does is make the right decision. It might not seem like the right decision is always obvious (and not always easy), but in the end, if the decision was made with the best interests of students and student achievement in mind, then it's the right decision.

Once this environment is created in which school leaders are emitting a constant aura of excellence, it becomes contagious. Staff, students, and parents will have learned a new standard of excellence is the expected standard.

Part of this system of excellence naturally lends itself to creating a higher sense of professionalism. The word *professional* is thrown around a lot, but schools have to demand and expect a higher presentation of self from leaders and staff. From the way people dress to their attitude and their work ethic, a sense of authority, care, and quality matters. The people who work in school districts have to show students, parents, and the community that professionalism is standard.

These expectations of professionalism then affect how people interact with their colleagues and then with students and parents. It is a domino system of reactions. As the leaders and teachers grow in quality of excellence and professionalism, the students begin to pick up on this. And then those students have a constant example of what is expected of them. Children learn what they see.

The expectation of professionalism applies to parents too. Half the battle is teaching parents how to act in school. As was mentioned before, as a generalization, parents who live in poverty tend not to trust the school system. Parents have to learn the appropriate channels in which to communicate and advocate. As parents learn to advocate for their child more professionally, with authority, care, and quality, the bond of trust grows.

So, how does a parent learn the appropriate way to communicate and advocate for his child? By thinking about himself as the child's first and most important teacher. By thinking of himself as a parent who wants what is best for his child just like the teachers do. When a parent thinks about himself as a teacher and an advocate, it creates a sense of teamwork. But to understand this, a parent has to trust that his child is going to the best school each day. Schools have to prove they are the best place for kids to be each day.

When schools have leaders and staff functioning at high levels of professionalism, care, and support, the parents begin to trust the system and learn to recognize the signs of a quality school. Parents are then able to talk with teachers and principals like they are on the same team. Parents truly just want to be told honestly how their child is maneuvering throughout the school day. Whether it's academically, socially, or emotionally, parents want to know that their child is making it through the day. Parents want to know their child is loved, taken care of, and respected. When these social and emotional aspects are secure, many obstacles to the academic portion are removed.

When a parent approaches a teacher or principal out of love and care, that parent will be met with understanding and support. Parents should always approach a teacher or principal in this spirit. First and foremost, this is the parent's job—loving, caring, and thinking about her child's life. Teachers and principals are intuitive when it comes to this idea. Schools know when parents are approaching them out of love and care versus haste and confrontation.

These are all notions that flow from knowing how to interact with people. When parents or schools don't know how to interact appropriately, then they have to be taught. Good people teach others how to be good people. The basic rule of treating each other how you would want to be treated reigns supreme in interacting with anyone. Schools have to help parents learn this. Teachers have to help parents learn this. As the saying goes, people don't care how much you know until they know how much you care.

By now, most educators know that the biggest indicator of successful students is a quality teacher. Think of this in two ways—a quality *classroom* teacher and a quality teacher (parent) at *home*. The biggest student gains happen when students have a quality teacher. Again, *the biggest student gains happen when students have a quality teacher.* This is a factor that schools have control over—who is teaching their students. Teachers are the largest part of the success equation. People who care and support and teach students each day are the biggest indicator of success. It's people.

Teachers have to deeply care about kids and their success. The core of what a teacher does each day has to come from a place of care and love, like a parent does, when she works with her students. This might be one of the only jobs that requires an employee to have that qualification. As a parent, knowing that your child is in an environment in which the teachers and principals genuinely care and support your child from a place of love has to be an overwhelmingly humbling feeling. This scenario works when the parties share a common expectation that only the best people are involved.

It should be an expectation that only the best people are involved in working with kids. The fight to ensure every teacher in a school is the best teacher possible for that classroom is a battle worth fighting. There has to be pressure on the weak links. Schools have to have a culture of rewarding and highlighting good teachers and good leaders. Teachers and leaders should be given this ultimatum: get on board or leave. Schools, parents, and students don't have time to waste dealing with ineffective people. Schools and communities need to feel a sense of urgency to skyrocket to the status of a top performing school system. It's not going to happen when the people on board aren't willing to work hard, work smart, and work together.

Educators should ask themselves this question: *Would I be comfortable with my child in this school?* If the answer is no, then the leaders and the staff are in charge of changing that. Leaders should be first and foremost phenomenal teachers. The primary responsibility of the leaders is to help teach teachers.

Leaders should know what is required from an exceptional teacher, and leaders should know how to help teachers become better. If an educator wouldn't feel comfortable with his own child in the school, then he, along with the rest of the school, is responsible for changing the environment. Educators have to provide the school opportunity that any child deserves.

Attending a high-performing school should be an opportunity that each child gets. Why aren't more people tuned in to the fact that some students aren't receiving the best education possible? People need to start going outside of their comfort zones in order to reach all students and their parents. *People* are the bridge to student achievement. Human connection is the bridge to student achievement.

Schools should make a human connection outside of school too. Know your students outside of school. Principals and teachers should go to a student's piano recital. They should call a parent at work just to say her child scored perfectly on her spelling test. Connections with students and parents solidify relationships. Make the connection in the moment.

Sometimes the little stuff matters more—like sending a condolence note when a student's family member dies. The students will know that their principals and teachers care about them with a professional, academic tone, and also on a personal level. The little things are notes, hand shakes, a wink, or one word of encouragement. People have to be personable. Students are people too—treat them as such.

And please send the best teachers to work with the most academically challenged students. The best teachers and best leaders get it. Build schools around the teachers and leaders who are the best; the best at making human connections and the best at teaching kids. Make it about people first.

Schools have to create a culture of *people first*. People—whether it's the teachers, parents, or students—have to be the priority, because it's the people who are going to produce results. It's a travesty for great teachers to support poor teachers and great leaders to support poor leaders. If you are a great leader and teacher, you should expect others to be great. Children of poverty will most likely never achieve in spite of their teachers and leaders. Teachers in these schools have to be exceptional.

When the best teachers and leaders are working in schools, they can encourage the parents to be exceptional as well. Once the best staff is in place, working with parents to help make them exceptional is easier.

Awesome, professional people in schools always reach out and make everyone else around them better. It's a natural action to help make the parents better teachers and advocates for their children.

When great teachers, principals, and leaders are involved, they begin to interact with parents in the spirit of partnership and teamwork. Teaching parents how to help create achieving students then becomes easier. Once parents have the trusting people part down, the part where they know that the people in their school are professional and loving and qualified, parents are ready for the academic part. They are ready to learn what makes a truly great school district.

Trust is built on proven reliability. When schools have the best people involved, then everyone can grow and succeed together, trusting that each person (whether parent or teacher) is worthy of the effort.

Chapter summary: Schools can't achieve positive, stunning results without great people working in them. Schools also can't produce amazing results without the help from parents. Parents have to be the people children need them to be. They have to be exceptional parents who send their kids to schools full of exceptional teachers and leaders. Good people in schools can help parents learn how to be good parents. Mutual respect, professionalism, and quality should all be part of what the people in schools share. Whether the people are teachers, leaders, students, or parents, each should have the characteristics of what it means to be a good person. Schools and parents have to learn that it's *people first*.

THREE

What Makes a Good School District Great?

Strong academics make a good school district great. Academics are the leveler of the playing field. Only when a school district proves it can successfully deliver rigorous academics for all students can it be considered a great school district.

What makes a good school district a great school district? Lots of things. First and foremost, there has to be a starting point in trying to get better. Assess where you are and where you want to be.

Start with this premise: this school district is a good school district, but it is going to be a great (high-performing) school district. Every school district has good qualities. Even the struggling school districts have some redeeming qualities. There might be just a few, but if you look hard enough, you will always find something good.

Whether it is an outstanding teacher, or a caring principal with the right intentions, or beautiful facilities, or active parent participation, or a neighborhood clean-up event, there are always good things happening in school districts. People don't choose education as a career to be terrible teachers or principals and fail students.

Starting with the premise that a school district is a good school district makes everyone focus on what really is going well. However, this premise also forces a school district to focus on what is not going well.

When school leaders analyze the things that are going well in their schools, it produces a list of positive items to include in the school's message. This message is so important to start helping the school shape its internal and external perception. Schools have to build on the positives, and the positive connotations have to permeate to the staff and then to the parents and community. The positive things happening in schools will help contribute to the vision of the school. This vision has to be shared with parents, students, and the community.

Ideally, the list of things that are going well in a school district includes high expectations and advanced academics, but if these are items that need to be enhanced, then the school district has to be honest about needing to be better and work harder at producing advanced academic students. The honest answer at this point is that *we have work to do*. This then becomes a goal and a message—that the school district has some good qualities, but it also has work to do to become a high-achieving school district.

This acknowledgment of having to get better (every school district can always be better) helps build the message around high expectations. Leaders set the tone for the message and image of the school district, and it's important to think about the brand at this point. A school district's brand is the overall feeling that people think about when they see your name.

What do people think about your school district's brand? What is the initial reaction from people when your school district is mentioned? The goal is for the answer to be associated with connotations of high academic performance.

From the superintendent to the public information officer to each central office administrator, each building principal, and the staff of each school, the people must unrelentingly focus on the message of *performance*. If someone doesn't believe in the message of academic performance, then that person does not fit in the school. This also applies to parents. Parents have to learn the message too. Parents have to know that the vision, message, and brand includes them. Parents need to have the same expectations of themselves—that of accepting nothing but the best in how they communicate and advocate for the schools and for their child.

Everyone is a communicator. Everyone shapes the message and changes the perception. Everyone has to adjust to the message and preach the message of high expectations with the vision of advanced academic achievement.

This message of performance has to permeate all levels of the school district. High expectations include not only high academic achievement but also the very best effort from each program and staff member. Make each person working in the school district feel like it's their responsibility to perform at a high level in each aspect of his or her job. From relating to students to sending e-mails to greeting guests at events to working with the custodial staff, expect nothing but the best from staff, teachers, and leaders. This expectation will begin to police itself once the belief is instilled in the school.

As expectations filter throughout the school, parents and students will start to notice. Parents, isn't it refreshing to walk into a school that feels like excellence? Isn't it refreshing to feel a sense of pride and professionalism when you approach people working in your schools? Isn't it reassuring to be greeted by the principal at every school event? These kinds of feelings that parents have when they walk into their child's school are intangible. These are feelings that cannot be bought or handed out.

Leaders should help cultivate these feelings in parents by always being present at school events. Leaders have to be the face of the school. This builds upon the brand and the message that the leaders care about how they are perceived and how the district is perceived. It shows a sense of caring about what a school looks like to parents and guests.

Parents will embrace a school that makes them feel important and worthy. Parents love to feel like their child's school values them as well. Schools, be very intentional about how you make your parents feel. Schools should not let the opportunity to make parents feel like part of the school go unattended. These parents' thoughts and emotions about how they feel when they walk into their child's school can help propel the partnership even further. If unattended, schools have an uphill battle in winning partners in student achievement.

The feelings that both parents and teachers feel about a school drives the message coming out of a school. An environment of good vibes fuels positive attitudes about everyone working together to spread the message of expectations and performance.

Part of the message-grinding effort includes working with media outlets. Whether a school district is in a big market with several news affiliates, or in a small market with maybe only a local newspaper, there is always an outlet to report the news. With blogs, e-newsletters, Twitter,

Facebook, websites, and so forth, news is easier than ever to disseminate. It's also easier than ever for news to get out of control.

Embrace this cycle of media madness. Make informing contacts at the newspaper and local television news outlets part of the school district's spirit. Keep the local mommy blogger informed. Keep the local city council and business community informed. Invite parents to help in this effort. Use parents as tools to spread the good news. Empower parents to be spokespeople for the district. And when parents feel a strong connection to their child's school, they should want to help spread the good news. The more people (teachers and parents in the community) who are on your side of the message, the better chance you have of maintaining the message you want spread.

In sticking with the message of improving *performance* unrelentingly, the so-called "bad news" is kept minimal. It is the school district's job to help the media and public understand that the petty, scrappy things are not newsworthy or important. It is essential that schools shift from reporting on fundraisers and neighborhood fights to academic, performance-oriented stories all the time. All news should be about positive, academic-related projects.

Minimum standards cannot be good enough anymore. This has to be at the heart of improving and at the heart of communication with the public. Good enough is no longer really *good enough*. The news has to be elevated to make the public think about what really matters for schools. Most parents will say that their school district is good, but ask them what they think about the school district down the street and you might get a different answer.

Why is this? Why do parents think that their child's school district is better than another? Because school districts don't do a good job of elevating the conversation to be wholly about positive, academic-related stories at all times. Sure, schools need to talk about the human angle of emotion and students who are great kids, but that will come naturally out of stories that originate from high achievement. Elevating the conversation about schools is everyone's job. When the school district learns to maintain the conversation focus on high standards, the parents learn how to follow that lead. Schools must start leading the way in this conversation. And it has to be done by proving itself academically.

The motto "Failure is not an option" has circulated around education circles over the past few years. Failure is indeed not an option. Schools and parents should put a laser-like focus on and prioritize expectation of success. This buy-in from everyone seems to happen when the conversation starts to tip in the direction of success.

There is a tipping point when all the news and talk coming from a school district is swayed in one direction: the direction of performance and success. This is when a call from the local television news outlet becomes a call seeking advice and expert opinion on school achievement. This is when a call from a parent becomes a call congratulating the school district on the outstanding test scores printed in the newspaper. This is when a call from the chief executive officer of a Fortune 500 company becomes a call offering a check to help support science and math classrooms. This is when a call from the commissioner of education becomes a call asking for help in working with other school districts. The tipping point slants in the direction of success when the conversation is focused on academic rigor.

Good enough cannot be good enough anymore. School districts have to be great. Parents have to be great. There are too many students and parents who need extra support and guidance. Great schools are everyone's business. There is too much at stake for schools and parents to sit on the sidelines while others flounder around in districts that aren't cutting it. *Good enough cannot be good enough anymore.* A great school district elevates other school districts. It starts with one. It starts with yours.

Chapter summary: There are all kinds of messages that come from schools—messages of instructions, activities, news, fundraisers, and students. In the whirl of noise that comes from schools, schools have to be very intentional about making sure the message they are sending is about performance and student achievement. Nothing else matters if the academics suffer. Talk about performance and student achievement as the only things that matter in creating a great school district. Make every school and every parent sing the tune of student achievement. Soon, when the message is focused on performance, the song sounds the same and everyone knows what the goal is.

FOUR
What Are Our Students Like Today?

If great school districts have to start helping elevate subpar school districts, then part of the conversation is going to have to involve talking about students. What are students like today?

In enrollment numbers, students look like this:

- There are approximately 13,600 public school districts made up of over 98,800 public schools in the United States.
- In the fall of 2012, over 49.8 million students attended public elementary and secondary schools. Of these, 35.1 million were in pre-kindergarten through eighth grade, and 14.8 million were in grades 9–12.
- About 1.3 million children were enrolled in public pre-kindergarten in 2012. Enrollment in kindergarten was approximately 3.7 million students.
- In the fall of 2012, about 4 million public school students enrolled in the ninth grade—the typical entry grade for many American high schools.[1]

Demographically, students look like this:

- In 2008, the US Census Bureau reported that elementary and high school students today were more diverse by race or Hispanic origin than the baby boom generation of students.
- In 1970, when the crest of the baby boom generation was in elementary and high school, the student population was 79 percent non-Hispanic white, 14 percent black, 1 percent Asian and Pacific

islander and other races, and 6 percent Hispanic.
- In 2008, 59 percent were non-Hispanic white, 15 percent were black, 5 percent Asian, and 18 percent Hispanic.[2]

Now consider this:

- Using 2005 figures, the Population Reference Bureau estimates that about 45 percent of children younger than five years of age are minorities.
- In 2010, 21.6 percent of children under the age of eighteen lived in poverty.
- The percentage of births to unmarried mothers has nearly doubled since 1990, up from 26.6 percent that year to 40.6 percent in 2008.[3]

Students today are more diverse by race and origin than the students from the baby boom generation. Even though students may look different or come from different situations, the approach to working with all students still has to come from a place of love, support, and high performance. Every child wants to be loved and nurtured and respected for who they are, no matter what their life situation is.

Students today may have more mobile devices, video games, and distractions than ever before, but that does not take away the fact that they still need and want the same things the kids from earlier generations needed and wanted. The simple, qualitative things like love, support, kindness, help, encouragement, trust, honesty, and someone to care about them are what kids need and want. They also need adequate shelter, clothing, and nourishment.

A good place to begin when creating systems of supports for students is by starting with the realization that kids these days are similar to kids of days gone by in regards to what they want and need emotionally. Students want extra support and they want people who care about them in their lives. Parents and schools have to give it to them.

Think about the student who comes from a nuclear family consisting of a mother, father, and siblings. Let's say this student is a girl who is in high school. She makes good grades, is in advanced placement courses, plays soccer, has parents who cheer for her and encourage her, and is on her way to college and career. Then think about another student who comes from a family of divorced parents. She has the same qualities as the girl from the nuclear family (but maybe she plays basketball instead of soccer). Then think about another student who lives with his grandparents, makes good grades, has excellent attendance, and participates in choir and debate. Think about another student who comes from a single-parent home, makes good grades, has excellent conversation skills, reads at a high level, and is ready for high school.

On the other hand, think about all these situations with different characteristics. Maybe the girl doesn't get good grades because she lives in a car with her mom and dad and siblings on the weekends. Maybe the other girl who has divorced parents isn't supported in her studies because her mom is busy finding drugs and drinking alcohol. Maybe the boy who lives with his grandparents doesn't go to school and has poor attendance because his clothes don't look right. Or maybe the student from the single-parent home is late for school each day and lags two years behind in reading levels.

The common factor in these scenarios is that each student is a kid just trying to make it in the school setting. What parents and educators do with each of these students will look a bit different, but the goal of addressing each of them as individuals with a need of support and encouragement remains a constant. The support, encouragement, and love just gets processed by each student differently.

As parents, this is a good reminder as well. Your children need your support, encouragement, and love, but they may need it delivered in different ways. All kids have differences in how they want to get hugged or high-fived or rewarded. Adults have to figure out how kids want to receive the recognition and support. As babies, children are too young to tell you, but they cry, coo, and smile. Adjusting to these baby signals happens fairly quickly when the parent responds appropriately. As the baby gets older, parents learn how to adapt to cues from their children faster and better. Sometimes as parents it feels like the whole day is made up of responding to a child's needs, which then turns into weeks and then into months. As the years pass, parents are still always meeting their child's needs, but it looks different as their kids grow up.

Meeting a child's needs is not just a parent's job, though; it also becomes the school's job. With the onslaught of differentiated instruction and individualized instruction, there are many tools to help meet diverse student needs. This essentially means that different ways of teaching are used to teach different types of students. Maybe a student can't hear in the back of the class, so the teacher moves him to the front. Maybe a student loves to read nonfiction books about owls, so the teacher finds as many books about owls as he can and provides those as homework. Maybe a student learns through group work better than solitary work, so the teacher uses group roles more often. Maybe a student learns by reading an instruction manual and can automatically convert those instructions to building a robot, so the teacher lets her work alone with a robot kit during reading time.

Whatever the student need and interest level, this is where the teacher (and parent) should meet the student. However, there is a fine line between meeting a student at her academic and interest level and also pushing her to strive to reach the next level. This is the art of teaching and parenting. This art of teaching and parenting, though, also has to have a mix of fun, play, laughter, seriousness, nurturing, love, and support.

Volunteer and mentor programs consistently find that when a group of young people are surveyed and asked about additional things they want out of their school experience, students say they want extra adults in their lives who support and care about them. This speaks to the heart of what educators and parents do each day. Educators and parents are adults who care about kids and support kids. Recruit more of these adults and form a volunteer program with them. Add to your army of people supporting students.

Think about a student named Joe who had a volunteer. Let's call the volunteer "David." Joe doesn't have a stable father figure in his life, so David volunteers to spend time with Joe during the school day as a mentor. Joe and David meet when Joe is in third grade. As Joe moves through the grade levels, through elementary school, middle school, and high school, David is there each year as an encouragement and a friend.

Joe and David form a friendship that lasts through Joe's senior year, when David helps Joe apply for colleges and scholarships. This relationship transforms how Joe sees adults in his life. This relationship also shows David that helping a student is the best part of his day—that giving time to a student is the best internal reward as a volunteer.

Joe goes to college, meets a girl, falls in love, and proposes to her. David is the first person Joe calls to share the news. Joe then asks David to be his best man in the wedding. This is what it means to build a school of students who have extra support people. This is what it means to surround students with love and care. Provide opportunities for adult mentors to form friendships with students. In the best cases, you might even get a story like Joe and David's.

When students feel supported and loved, they will work hard to prove themselves to adults. As educators, it's important to use this to the students' benefit. By creating systems of recognitions and systems of academic and emotional support for students, a school sets up a system for producing students that feel valued and worthy. The students' responsibility is going to school to learn and achieve each day. When they feel like school is a worthy endeavor, they will work hard to uphold that notion. So schools have to create an environment that is geared toward making students feel good about student accomplishments. This is a sense of pride.

This sense of pride in a school seems to grow on its own as the environment shifts to an environment of support, worthiness, and high expectations. Students start to check up on each other. They start to be interested in others feeling worthy, smart, and excellent. Just like when the teachers start to monitor each other, the students do the same thing.

Think about how wonderful it is when teachers and students create an environment of mutual respect and appreciation. Schools and parents should cultivate this feeling each day. This is when recognition and rewards for academic excellence and good citizenship come into play. Setting up a system of recognitions for students, based on what students think is important, helps motivate students. Is it buying lunch for students prepping for the ACT? Is it paying for students to take dual-credit courses in conjunction with the local university? Is it bringing in a concert for students who earn the right to attend? Is it giving out a T-shirt that the students designed?

There are unlimited ideas for rewarding students, but before the rewards start, students have to first understand the idea of being accountable for their own learning. Students have to be accountable for their own progress. This idea of student responsibility mirrors the idea of a child's responsibility at home. When kids are given the chance to be responsible for themselves, they usually do a great job of it.

The innate feeling of being accountable and responsible for ourselves flourishes when the opportunity presents itself over and over. Think about toddlers wanting to do almost everything for themselves—feeding themselves, pouring cereal from the cereal box, drinking out of a big cup without a lid, gluing a card shut, painting without help, digging in the dirt, and the list goes on. They want to do it all by themselves. This doesn't change as kids get older.

When students are given the opportunity to track their own learning and progress, they seem to do better. This is because they see their own stake in the game. Schools and parents have to give this opportunity to students. Schools and parents have to provide opportunities for students to see how they are doing and where they are going. Knowing the goal is important.

So not only knowing the path of accountability but also knowing the end goal promotes a natural system of achievement. When students know the path they have to take to get to a stated goal, they tend to do better. Why wouldn't teachers and parents provide this system around students?

Accountability and responsibility are nice to think about in theory. But really, using this in practice requires students who move around in a school feeling good about the other students there. There is beauty in diversity and there is beauty in students who appreciate each other. This beauty is innate in kids. Kids do not notice the difference between other kids except in maybe color of skin or accent or language. Even then, that quality is not seen as a difference, but it is seen as another characteristic out there in the world. Can you imagine if that sense carried throughout their lives? This is what kids want to keep alive—the sense of acceptance and nonchalance about all kinds of people.

Kids want honesty. They need honesty at their level. And they know when someone is not telling the truth. Again, there is beauty in all kinds of students learning and teaching each other. Students appreciate this in schools where this feeling of beauty and diversity is cultivated. It produces students who care about each other and care about their school. It then produces students who care about how they are seen from the outside. Getting students to understand how they are perceived helps them to understand that they have to prove themselves even more. It produces achievement because it forces students to think about themselves in a higher capacity.

Students have the sense of feeling responsible and accountable for themselves, but now they have it to a greater degree because it matters how they are perceived, not only individually but also collectively. Students thinking about each other collectively. Imagine that! Then imagine whole school systems, whole cities, whole states, and whole nations thinking about each other collectively.

Chapter summary: Our students are more diverse today than ever. Embrace the reality and teach students with love, care, respect, and expectations. The diversity and reality of what our students carry as baggage and weight on their shoulders is not going away. What *can* go away, though, is the attitude that *these students* can't learn and can't handle it in school. Students have proven over and over again that when they are treated as individuals who need love, support, and goals, they rise to the challenge. Schools should wrap students up in a security blanket and nurture their learning at high levels. Parents should do the same.

There are 50 million students in public education in this country. These 50 million students have parents. So, let's say there are at least 100 million people in the United States who have a direct stake in how students learn. Then add in all the teachers, principals, and staff in schools. This makes the number of people in this country who have a direct stake in education grow exponentially. These numbers make up more than half of the US population.

Education is something that each of the more than 300 million people in the United States should care about. Why aren't more people thinking about the 50 million students and what they deserve?

NOTES

1. "U.S. Department of Education, National Center for Education Statistics," nces.ed.gov (August 2013).

2. "The United States of Education: The Changing Demographics of the United States and Their Schools," centerforpubliceducation.org (August 2013).

3. Ibid.

FIVE
Relationships and Responsibility

Thinking about each other collectively means thinking about relationships and responsibility. It's everyone's job to be responsible for each other. As parents, we can think about it in the realm of *it takes a village to raise a child*. As schools, we can think about it as succeeding or failing together.

There is a word on the island of Okinawa, Japan, called *monchu*. Keep in mind that the island of Okinawa is known for having the largest number of elderly residents per capita in the world, which means that their island is known for longevity of life. This word *monchu* means "one family." It's a feeling of everyone on the island being part of the same family. It's also a feeling of everyone on the island being responsible for each other. From young to old, each resident is responsible for teaching (and reminding) the lessons of youth and age. Maybe there is a correlation between togetherness and longevity, or between responsibility and success. It's everyone's job.

Schools have to create an environment in which leaders, teachers, students, and parents feel responsible for the success of the school. This is creating a sense of empowerment for them to always make the right decisions based on the good of the school and the students. A feeling of responsibility is a feeling of purpose.

Within responsibility lies relationships. If responsibility is a sense of purpose, then relationships are what will make a school thrive. Relationships between leaders and teachers, teachers and students, and schools and parents (and any combination of those) have to be successful for academic goals to be met. Relationships build a system in which leaders, teachers, students, and parents have multiple supports, and in which students feel like they have multiple people, within the school and even outside the school, holding them up and supporting them.

The system of relationships—having many people caring about many others—helps students see collaboration, professionalism, and learning. Students see how important they are in the equation. If done right, students get the benefit of positive relationships because it becomes all about making students feel valued and important.

Think about inviting parents and other outside adults into schools on a regular basis. Whether it's a volunteer program through which caring adults work regularly with kids in schools or businesses that sponsor a group of students for a project, it's part of building relationships to have these external groups working with students. Getting students in front of corporate business leaders and volunteers makes students feel like they are part of the conversation about the future. And it again promotes that extension of themselves—that feeling that they have to work on how they are perceived in the community.

Students have to build on these kinds of experiences in their lives in order to build upon their outlook on life. The exposure to relationships within their school and within their community adds to their life view. The exposure to quality, meaningful relationships makes students' worlds bigger. It also puts their lives into perspective.

In this digital age, stop and ponder the art of relationships and conversation. To make a student's life bigger and more meaningful, he is going to have to have the skills to relate and converse with all kinds of people. In schools, in the workforce, and in a social setting, kids have to navigate these settings with confidence and experience. These kinds of situations lend themselves to relationship-building and collaborative skills.

Teach students and parents about relationships by writing personal, handwritten notes to them. Teach them about caring by modeling caring. Teach them about relationships by being a good support and listener. Teach them about the real world by hosting businesses for lunch in the schools. All of these things build relationships—both internally and externally.

While building the relationships within school walls is important, it's also important to build relationships with the local community. Inviting businesses and local community leaders into schools helps them to understand what happens in schools. Put the students in front of these community leaders so that the leaders can see what their future workforce and city will look like. The leaders should have a large stake in the students' outcomes because the students are going to be the leaders' future workforce.

It is priceless to see a Fortune 500 company chief executive officer speak in front of a group of students. This executive may get deferential treatment from other adults, but when working with kids, no question or comment is off the table. Having a professional executive interact with kids in schools and be silly and honest about the workforce helps to make connections that won't necessarily impact her company's bottom line, but will have an impact on her credibility in the community. Make these connections part of a school's routine and part of the students' interactions.

The school leadership team and staff has to be professional and inviting to the community and business leaders. Make it easy to work with the schools. Make it feel productive and proactive. Community and business leaders should want to work schools because schools make it easy for those leaders to feel like they are part of something successful and special. That sense of pride that the students and teachers built can now cascade into making community leaders feel good about the schools too.

There are unlimited ways to make the community feel good about their relationship with the schools, but always think about ways to foster this sense of connection. Maybe have students canvass the neighborhood to talk about a school project or distribute school information. Organize neighborhood cleanup events to show that students care about where they go to school and what it looks like. Host district nights when the whole community is invited to the stadium for a carnival, free food, and free admittance to the football game. The activities and events hosted by the school should have a connection to helping the community. Show your community that its schools are here for them, that the schools are here to build relationships.

The circle of relationships and responsibility doesn't end with direct school-to-community connection. It also includes schools working with other schools to build relationships of collaboration. Think about the highest-achieving school mixing with the lowest-achieving school. By association, the lower-performing students should be elevated by working with the higher-achieving students. The expectations floating in the air should be normalized to fit to the higher-achieving students. It is a situation in which *better students make better students*; therefore, while each school has a responsibility to itself to be successful, it also has a responsibility to other schools to ensure that they succeed as well.

Is this a radical view of collectivism? No, it's simply the hard truth that if our schools are going to be successful, then the leaders, teachers, students, and parents who are high performing and successful are going to have to help those leaders, teachers, students, and parents who are not to become better. It's the spirit of our nation to fight the good fight and buck the systems of conventionalism. What a great system to fight for—the system of our schools! If not for the 50 million students, their parents, and their schools, then who else are we going to fight for?

Chapter summary: The days of thinking that it is someone else's responsibility to educate and take care of our students is over. It's everyone's responsibility. The schools in this country, and especially the schools of poverty and diversity, have to become the responsibility of everyone. The leaders, teachers, parents, and students who know what it takes to succeed have to teach the schools and parents who don't know the path to success what it takes. Schools are too important to fail. Students are everyone's responsibility. It takes a village to raise our kids, and the village boundaries are increasingly fluid. Everyone's backyard has students who need help.

SIX
Having Quality Systems

When the word *fight* is mentioned, it's not intended to stir up a real fisticuffs-type fight, but it is intended to stress the importance of addressing a real issue head-on. But if the word *fight* were taken in a literal sense, then let's talk about schools being the opposite of conflict by being safe havens for students and the community. Schools have to create systems of attention to detail—systems that go above and beyond to show that schools care about where their students, parents, and staff congregate each day and night.

Systems are an approach to running a school. Systems are the functional parts of schools. The functional parts of schools have to be well greased and able to operate at high levels.

The perception of public schools being systems full of delinquent, rough kids exists in some parent and community mindsets. While this perception holds true in some schools that do not have the systems in place to correct this issue, it's a nonissue in most public schools. Yes, public schools have to take every student within their boundaries, and yes, that does mean schools have kids who don't have the appropriate responses and skills to act mannerly and respectfully. But it also means that schools and parents have to start doing a better job of raising our kids well.

There are schools that are rough, that are unsafe. But these schools are really in the minority. It is imperative that the unsafe schools are cleaned up to be safe schools because safe schools are the rock of the community. Schools have to be a place of refuge and comfort for kids, as well as a place for learning. It is unacceptable to have a school that is not safe. Working on safe schools should be a priority for everyone.

Parents who don't have experience with unsafe schools generally don't understand the factors that lead to unsafe schools. It only takes a small, false, urban legend–type incident to become the blown-out-of-proportion scary story that parents and the community think about as an indicator of the safety of a certain school. With this, it's small fights and kids acting inappropriately that seem to overshadow the positive news that happens the overwhelming majority of the time. The fix is this: Don't let the small fights and inappropriate behavior happen, and when it does, don't let it become the focus of what you're doing. Correct the behavior, have a zero-tolerance approach to violence, and move forward.

This is certainly a highly sensitive issue, especially when thinking about the devastating and incomprehensible violence that school shootings elicit. But the internal safety that is controllable (to a certain extent) in schools, has to be a priority for schools. Toward this end, safe, orderly schools start with consistent discipline, strong relationships, facility management, and well-run events and activities.

In a nutshell, the zero-tolerance approach and the safe schools act is this: Under no circumstances can a student, employee, or guest in a school have unsafe items or exhibit unsafe behaviors that could harm another person. If so, this is grounds for expulsion, suspension, and/or criminal charges.

Safety is a priority. Safety is a basic need that needs to be met before any learning can take place—let alone high achievement. The people (parents, school leaders, teachers, counselors, students, community leaders) are in charge of this. Responsibility and relationships are in charge of this. Safety is a priority. Only safe and orderly schools can produce the kind of environment needed to have achieving students.

Once the safety of a school is addressed and made right, there are some natural functions that also have to happen in schools. Having functional systems of attention to detail contribute to the feeling of safety in a school.

You never want guests, and those in the community who would otherwise have no contact with your schools, to have a chance to say something negative about your schools.

Marquees, signs, and banners at schools have to be current, and they must convey messages that are relevant. This might be the only contact that someone in the community has with a school. What does your school marquee say right now? What is the message you are trying to share? What image are you trying to convey?

The perception of the schools by those who live in the community starts with appearance. The grounds have to be free of litter and well landscaped. The parking lots have to be clean. Hallways have to be trash free. These items are important when guests (and parents) enter school buildings and immediately judge the school based upon how it looks.

Do the buildings' grounds look like a stereotypical urban school? Do they look rundown and neglected? Or do they look like a manicured safe haven from suburbia dropped in the middle of the city? All schools should look like the latter. In fact, school districts should expect to spend time and money beautifying their schools. The look of a school is a big indicator in how it's perceived and judged. *Don't judge a book by its cover?* You know you do—everyone does.

Then go beyond the school grounds. How do the sidewalks look along the streets leading to your schools? In need of repair? Nonexistent? The look and feel of the neighborhoods surrounding the schools should be held to the same high standards of the schools' grounds. A school's image does not end at its property line. Schools encroach upon the whole neighborhood if done correctly. This means the school's appearance, cleanliness, and pride should start to affect how the neighborhood feels about its own homes, sidewalks, and streets.

If the sidewalks and streets are in need of repair, partner with the city and get it done. Use the city resources and use the elected officials to work in the school's favor. Create a pipeline of communication with city administrators to work on the neighborhoods around the schools. Help the city administrators understand the work that needs to be done and why it affects the schools. The city will earn praise for its attention to the areas around schools, and the schools will gain safer, beautiful streets and sidewalks. Both the city and the schools win.

Make the neighborhoods part of the school's responsibility. Does the principal drive through her neighborhoods and know where students and parents live? Do the parents feel like the school has an open-door policy? Does this partnership go both ways? Can the principal walk into a family's home and feel welcome? This open door policy continues to build on the relationships and trust factor. It creates a system of partnership, of looking out for each other in the neighborhood and in the school.

Systems of attention to detail in safety and in the look of schools should be part of the school's daily rhythm. By providing learning experiences, activities, and events that all contain the same standard of safety and care, schools ensure that each part of the whole always focuses on quality, functional systems.

Do events and activities start on time? Does the audience respect the presentation? Do the presenters respect the audience? Are the events well run? Are they meaningful and do they represent student achievement? When parents, guests, students, and community members come into your school, does the event's environment portray a feeling of success? This is a system that is created. It's a system that has to be cognizant in a school's psyche. Events and activities contribute to the whole picture of what a school looks like.

Not only is the appearance of a school important, but so is how it *sounds*. Have you ever thought about that before? When you walk into your school, whether you are a parent or a school employee or a guest, what does it sound like? Is it quiet? Is there a buzz of excitement? Is it peaceful? The sound should be reflective of the mood of the building. Systems of quiet hallways, peaceful transitions, energy, students learning, and teachers teaching will all affect the sounds of a school. Be aware of what your school sounds like.

How a school is viewed is affected by how it is presented to the public. Parents have to understand this too. What systems are the parents responsible for? Parents are responsible for holding up the same high standards that the school has. Do the moms gossip about teachers and other kids? Do the parents tell the school how to operate? Or is it a system that fosters collaboration and teamwork in its approach to helping kids?

Is the parent-teacher association a social gathering or a working meeting? (It can be both, but productivity is the key.) Do the parents take care of other parents? Meaning, do parents welcome new parents, teach new parents the expectations of performance, and show other parents what it means to be part of the system?

The point is that parents have to uphold the standard as well. Professionalism and respect to systems goes both ways. When both schools and parents are working at quality systems together, it shows.

It shows when everyone works together. Knowing a role in a system and then making that role useful to the function of a school helps parents and schools understand that both are important. Systems of roles and jobs help clearly identify responsibilities. Systems make schools run. Quality systems make quality schools, and both parents and schools are responsible for that.

Chapter summary: Safe schools full of people who care about functional systems and appearance should be standard in any school, but especially in urban schools. Urban schools have to work harder to ensure the perception and the reality of safety and quality are ingrained in the community. All of the suggestions in this chapter probably seem like little things that just add to everyone's daily regimen. They might appear tedious. But it's these seemingly little nuances that make the difference between good and great. They make the difference in how people view your schools.

Systems of relationships, rules, activities, authority, and behaviors have to be established, and they must exhibit stellar qualities of professionalism. Create systems of safety and activities that make schools the cherished grounds they are meant to be.

SEVEN
The Academic Standards

Both parents and schools are responsible for quality schools. The previous chapters covered that. The previous chapters have also outlined the characteristics of what schools have to do to achieve cultures and environments of success. The focus on early learning, people, the message, relationships and responsibility, students, and systems contributes to making schools places of success. When those characteristics are present, it opens the door to focus on the academics. In the end, it's the *academics* that are going to be the measuring stick to which all other parts of the school are compared.

Schools do a great job teaching kids. Every day schools teach kids all kinds of skills—reading, writing, math, science, art, music, fun, play, social/emotional; the list is endless. It's taking all of these skills and focusing on the essentially important ones that are converging to make schools what they are today. More than ever, parents and schools know how valuable time is. Focusing on the key items academically that are going to produce high-achieving students has become the goal. Also more than ever, parents and schools want a specific guidebook on how to do that.

By using the growth and success of the foundation built from the characteristics in the previous chapters, schools can turn that growth into the positive sentiment needed to influence parents to help improve schools. Schools cannot do it alone. Parents cannot do it alone. Schools and parents are going to have to achieve it together.

Schools should always maintain the focus of rigor and high performance. But schools don't always do a good job of explaining what *rigor* means, or what *performance* means. Rigor means having hard, strenuous, worthy, gut-wrenching, gifted academic material. It means having academic gusto. It means quality academics are everything. It means that kids' brains should hurt when they work on hard, meaningful academic projects. In that sense, the purpose of teaching and learning with students should be geared toward preparing them for college and career at a high level.

Montgomery County Public Schools in Rockville, Maryland, understand this concept. They compiled a list of the seven indicators that are essential to creating college-ready students. Based on their research, these are the seven criteria:

- Advanced Reading Grades K–2
- Advanced Reading Grades 3–8
- Advanced Math Grade 5
- Algebra I by Grade 8 (with a C or higher)
- Algebra II by Grade 11 (with a C or higher)
- 3 or better on AP Exam, 4 on IB Exam
- 24 on the ACT, 1650 on the SAT

These indicators are important to know, for they have been proven to show that when a student meets these seven steps, she is capable of being successful in college. These criteria identify several important components of academic success. They identify high academic benchmarks, and they also identify a commitment to constantly excelling. They show a commitment to perseverance. A student might be smart, but it takes applying the hard work necessary to meet these criteria throughout the K–12 experience that separates a successful college student from an unsuccessful one.

How do parents and schools know that their students are on track to meet these stepping-stones? Schools have to start helping students and parents by showing them the exact path needed to be prepared for college and careers when graduating from their district's high schools.

The Common Core State Standards outline the standards needed for students to be successful in a competitive, ever-evolving marketplace and world. The Common Core State Standards join states around the nation in the common goal of ensuring students are prepared for a rigorous future. Based on research and on input from teachers, parents, education leaders, and state leaders, the Common Core State Standards focus on the vitally important concepts and skills that students need to know when maneuvering through their school careers. In-depth information about the Common Core State Standards can be found at www.corestandards.org.

When students (and their parents) master the concepts contained within the Common Core State Standards, they will be on their way to college, ready for the demands that will be presented at the university level.

The Common Core State Standards start in kindergarten. But even before kindergarten, kids and parents have to work on certain areas to be ready for school. In the first chapter, the importance of early learning highlighted the word gap of kids who don't get exposed to reading, talking, listening, playing, and singing from birth. So, within this chapter, you will find the steps that parents need to follow even before school starts, as well as the exact standards needed to be successful.

The following guidelines are critical for parents (and their babies and preschoolers) to master even before kindergarten starts. This stage of learning almost solidifies the trajectory of success for a child. Whether good or bad, this early learning period will define how well a child does in school and is almost always a true predictor of success in the third grade. Meaning, if your child has the understanding of the foundational skills of vocabulary, books, play, interaction, pretend, and other infant-to-preschool skills prior to starting kindergarten, then he will virtually always be pegged to be a success in third grade and then beyond.

This may seem like a daunting and scary responsibility for parents and educators to absorb. But never fear! Most of the time these skills and the ways parents and educators interact with babies and early learners happen naturally. It's knowing when to be very intentional with babies and kids that makes the difference. Parents, your most important job is being a parent to your child. With this most important job, you have a responsibility to do some crucial things in raising your child. Educators, help the parents understand this truth.

The most important skills we can instill in young children are literacy skills. Literacy—encompassing reading, writing, speaking, and vocabulary—is the most essential key to success in school and beyond. Giving kids the power of literacy guarantees their ability to create their own path of learning at a high level. It's never too early to start.

So, if it's never too early to start, follow these guidelines from birth to make babies and toddlers ready for kindergarten.

BIRTH—SIX MONTHS: EMERGING

Talk

Everything about this world is a new experience for your baby. When you speak, your baby is fascinated. When she watches your mouth move, she is creating a framework of the language she will use for a lifetime. Make lots of time for face-to-face talking with your child. Narrate your actions. Expose your child to new vocabulary.

Cuddle

When you answer your baby's cries, you let him know that you understand his earliest communication. Let him know you are creating a safe, trustworthy, learning environment for him by taking lots of time to cuddle.

Read

Have books on hand. It's never too early to read to your baby. You are planting the seeds of language and literacy for a lifetime.

SIX TO FOURTEEN MONTHS: ON THE MOVE

Investigate

Your baby is moving around—which enables her to explore her world. Give her lots of room for free movement and place interesting, safe objects near her for her to discover. Prop some books open for her to investigate. She loves that she is now able to turn pages.

Experiment

Your baby is beginning to learn about cause and effect. Experimenting with rattles and other fun, safe toys that shake, drop, and bang are fun for your child. Experiment with opening and closing lids, placing items in and out of a box, and playing peek-a-boo.

Respond

Your baby wants to communicate with you! Even when he just babbles, take a minute to respond and have a miniconversation. Sometimes you can repeat the very sounds your child makes. This will reinforce sound awareness—a skill he will later use when learning to read.

Tip: Reading to your child every night before bedtime is one of the best things you can do as a parent to help her succeed in life and school.

FOURTEEN TO TWENTY-FOUR MONTHS: UNDERSTANDING

Narrate

Your baby is beginning to understand everything you say. To help him understand even more, *narrate* what's going on around him. As you talk about what is going on exactly as it happens, you help him match the words to the action or object they represent.

Stretch Talk

Her sentences will be very short—as short as one word. Help her develop language by stretching her ideas into a whole sentence. When she points and says, "Blankie," say, "Oh, you want to hold your blanket!" This is called stretch talk.

Be Understanding

Your child's understanding of language will far out-stretch his speaking abilities. This can be frustrating for him. Be patient. Some great bridges into spoken language are animal sounds, sounds in the world around us, and songs. Simple books with just a word or two on each page are valuable at this age. Toddlers often communicate with gestures. Let your child know you understand what he is trying to tell you.

Experience

Take your child around town—to the grocery store, the park, the post office. She will develop background knowledge that she will use later when she begins to read and write. These experiences help shape her understanding of the world around her.

TWENTY-FOUR MONTHS TO THREE YEARS: EXPRESSING

Restate Sentences

Your child is beginning to communicate fluently with you. Always take the time to answer his questions. As his grammar begins to develop, restate his sentences, but don't correct him. If he says, "Her take it," you reply, "Oh, she took the toy!"

Provide Opportunities to Read

Provide an abundance of rich literacy opportunities, such as pointing out environmental print (e.g., signs at stores and restaurants, labels of favorite foods, stop signs), books with repeating text that will be easy for your child to predict and memorize, and dialogic reading, which simply means discussing what is happening in a book. For instance, ask your child, "What do you think will happen next?" and "How do you think that child feels?" Use books and other opportunities to discuss conceptual language such as same and different, bigger and smaller.

Sing

Sing the alphabet song. Sing rhyming songs. Sing nursery rhymes. Play silly songs in your car and sing along with them. Sing and talk out loud every day. Create new songs. The sing-songy melodies help children learn and memorize words and sounds.

Draw

Your child will begin to express himself on paper. Encourage him daily to draw or write using a variety of materials. Occasionally, let him lie on his tummy and draw. This will help him develop a mature pencil grasp and develop a stronger body core.

Read, Read, Read

When you're reading to your child, point to the pictures. Talk about the pictures and what is happening in the book. Ask your child, "What do you think happens next? What is in this picture?" Allow your child to make predictions and direct the conversation. The conversation is often more important than the text.

Tip: Tell stories together. Make up silly stories and have your child fill in parts of the adventure. Pretend! Life is an adventure. Make your life with your child an adventurous journey that you navigate together. There is no better time than in childhood for humans to be unabashedly silly and creative. Use this time to foster that sense of adventure and wonder. It's also sentimental as adults to remember the feeling of inhibition and wonder. Try to see the world through your child's eyes.

THREE TO FIVE YEARS: CONTINUING THE LITERACY FOCUS

Read, Read, and Read Some More

When reading with your child, keep talking about what is happening in the book. And when finished with a book, ask your child, "What happened first in this book? What happened in the middle? And how did it end?" Ask your child to tell you her favorite part of the story. Ask her if it made any connections or reminded her of anything in her life.

Names

Your child should know his first and last name. Practice spelling it. Your child should also learn his parents' names.

Read a Variety of Books

Read all types of books—fiction, nonfiction, poetry, picture books, and so forth.

Rhyme Time

Read nursery rhymes and play rhyming games. Use time in the car or waiting in lines to make up words and rhyme them.

Handle with Care

Not only are you handling your child with care when you are sitting and reading together, but you are also showing your child how to take great care in respecting the process of reading. Teach your child to handle books with care: "This is the title page. This book was written by Dr. Seuss. Eric Carle drew the pictures." Close the book and say, "The end."

Encourage

Let your child read to you as best she can. Tell her, "You are a great reader!" Encourage your little reader and writer. Let your child be an author and create stories!

At this point, by working on the steps from birth to age five repeatedly, and with deep practice and fun, children will have a base for entering kindergarten. There are many important skills that a child needs when entering kindergarten. Are they high expectations? Yes, but these skills are going to put the child on a path toward other necessary benchmarks for being college-ready. Remember, it's never too early to start teaching and learning with children—the children who are going to be the students in our schools.

KINDERGARTEN READINESS SKILLS

Reading, Writing, Language, and Math

- Writes her own name and other meaningful words and phrases like *I love you*
- Begins to show interest in print rather than just pictures in books
- Knows letters and letter sounds
- Can recognize beginning sounds (*d* is for *dog*)
- Answers who, what, when, where, and how questions
- Retells stories
- Begins to decode simple words (*c-a-t* is *cat*)
- Shows interest in spelling and writing words
- Recites alphabet song and rhymes simple words
- Counts to twenty and recognizes numerals up to ten
- Understands that a numeral represents a quantity
- Understands directional/positional concepts (up, down, near, by)
- Uses descriptive words (hot, cold, most, least, day, night)
- Recognizes and names common shapes, colors, and body parts
- Follows multistep directions

Fine Motor

- Can use school supplies (scissors, crayons, pencils, glue, etc.)
- Draws simple shapes
- Can dress and undress (button, zip, etc.)

Gross Motor

- Has fun playing outside
- Jumps, hops, skips, gallops

Social and Emotional

- Expresses feelings through gestures, actions, and language
- Participates in relationships of mutual trust and respect
- Follows directions and acts in a safe and responsible way
- Shares and plays cooperatively with others
- Participates in conversations with adults and kids using complete sentences

By no means are these lists and tips all-inclusive, but they are a comprehensive overview of the skills parents should be teaching their kids and of the skills educators should be helping parents understand. There are always things parents can do to add depth and experience to the listed items, but the steps from birth that are outlined here are the basis for what parents should be focusing on. Parents are the best model for their kids. Deep modeling and deep practice of the key literacy steps outlined from birth to pre-kindergarten will be the start to advanced reading, advanced math, algebra, an ACT score above 24, and college.

Through these steps, parents are raising readers, writers, and thinkers. Students have to have the ability to struggle through problems and paragraphs and stories and then come out on the other end successfully. Students have to have what some people call *grit*. Grit is that internal struggle to do the right thing even though it may be hard. It's toughness. Grit can be taught, but it's taught when the foundation of literacy is ingrained in a student. Only then can a student think for himself, create for himself, struggle within himself, rationalize with himself, and then produce for himself.

Have you ever heard that FAIL stands for *First Attempt in Learning*? Giving a child the ability to reason, think, analyze, fail, and succeed is a gift that is not easily given. It is a gift that takes nurturing, time, persistence, toughness, and intentional action. Parents have to help other parents learn this gift. Why do so many parents float silently along when they can help shape all kids' learning?

Parents are the final frontier in helping schools reach the next level of achievement. We've got to get better together, and the birth to pre-kindergarten time period is the time to start molding that relationship of working together. By engaging parents and modeling to parents these foundational skills of literacy, schools are building its fleet of advanced students.

Schools, use the early learning program in your district to build your fleet. Use moms and dads to build your fleet. Parents need direction and support in raising babies and toddlers. It's hard work to be a parent. Schools can help influence these early years and help ease the burden of parents. Figure out who your army of people is that will go into these baby's homes and show their parents how to be a parent.

The vital role of parenting does not end though when a child gets to kindergarten. There exists a mentality of *now it's the school's job to teach and raise my child* when he gets to kindergarten. Yes, it's the school's job, but it's also the parents' job. Again, it's everyone's job.

Just as the school is going to track and keep up with a student's progress, so should the parent. Here are the steps (according to the Common Core State Standards) that students should master as they are on their path through elementary school. Parents and students both should be familiar with the following skills so that they know what is expected. Most times you can't win the game if you don't know how to play.

KINDERGARTEN

Smart Steps

- Designate a time for reading each day.
- Recognize rhyming words.
- Count syllables in big words.
- Read traffic signs and other environmental signs aloud.

Reading Goals: By the end of kindergarten, a child should be able to do the following (but is not limited to):

- Follow words from left to right, top to bottom, and page by page.
- Know all upper and lowercase letters of the alphabet.
- Recognize and produce rhyming words.
- Read common words by sight (*the, of, to, you*).
- Distinguish between similarly spelled words by noticing the sounds of the letters that differ and know basic sounds of each letter.
- Read emergent-reader and above texts with purpose and understanding.
- With prompt and support, identify main characters, settings, problems, and major events in a story.
- Write basic words to form a complete sentence.
- Know how to combine letters and make words.

Math Goals: By the end of kindergarten, a child should have the following skills (but is not limited to):

- Know number names and the count sequence.
- Count to tell the number of objects.
- Count aloud to 115.
- Understand addition as *adding to*.
- Understand subtraction as *taking from*.
- Classify and count the number of objects in a group (patterning and sorting).
- Tell time to the nearest hour.
- Describe, name, and interpret relative positions in space (above, below, in front, behind).
- Start to recognize and count money.

FIRST GRADE

Smart Steps

- Designate time for reading each night and discuss what was read.
- Practice a variety of ways to read known and unknown words.
- Practice vocabulary lists.
- Talk about how words are organized and used.

Reading Goals: By the end of first grade, a child should be able to do the following (but is not limited to):

- Recognize the distinguishing features of a sentence (first word capitalization, ending punctuation).
- Distinguish long from short vowel sounds in spoken single-syllable words.
- Know the spelling-sound correspondences for common consonant digraphs (two letters that represent one sound like *ch, sh, th*).
- Decode regularly spelled one-syllable words.
- Use knowledge that every syllable must have a vowel sound.
- Read grade-level and above-grade-level text with purpose and understanding.
- Describe characters, settings, problems, and major events in a story using key details.
- Write a paragraph with a minimum of four complete sentences.

Math Goals: By the end of first grade, a child should have the following skills (but is not limited to):

- Solve problems involving addition and subtraction.
- Extend patterns and describe how simple repeating patterns are generated.
- Count by twos, fives, and tens.
- Understand place value.
- Add and subtract for sums up to twenty.
- Measure lengths and compare it to real-world items ("this table is five pencils long").
- Tell and write time to the nearest hour and half hour.

SECOND GRADE

Smart Steps

- Designate time for reading each night.
- Ask your child questions before, during, and after reading a book with him.
- Have your child tell a story using details about a recent activity.
- Ask your child to tell you what time it is.
- Put a daily routine in place.

- Let your child check out a small amount of groceries at the store and discuss prices as you select and pay for the items.

Reading Goals: By the end of second grade, a child should be able to do the following (but is not limited to):

- Read grade-level and above-grade-level text with purpose and understanding.
- Ask and answer questions about an informational text they've read.
- Recount stories and determine a central message, lesson, or moral.
- Compare and contrast two or more versions of the same story.
- Describe the structure of the story (beginning, middle, and end).
- Ask your child to explain the meaning of a passage by *reading between the lines*.
- Write two or more paragraphs using five to seven sentences.

Math Goals: By the end of second grade, a child should have the following skills (but is not limited to):

- Represent and solve problems involving addition and subtraction.
- Recognize fractions, and use a variety of strategies to solve problems (such as using factors—ones, tens, hundreds).
- Measure and estimate lengths in standard units (inches, feet, centimeters, and meters).
- Work with time and money.
- Use manipulatives to recognize and represent shapes from different perspectives.

THIRD GRADE

Smart Steps

- Designate time for homework and reading each night.
- Describe how parts of a story build on one another.
- Share the point of view of the author of the story.
- Use a ruler to measure items up to the nearest 1/2 and 1/4 inch.

Reading Goals: By the end of third grade, a child should be able to do the following (but is not limited to):

- Identify and know the meaning of common prefixes and suffixes.
- Read grade-level and above-grade-level text aloud with accuracy and appropriate rate and expression, adjusting reading rate to the level of difficulty.
- Use context to confirm or self-correct word recognition and understanding, rereading as necessary.
- Ask and answer questions to demonstrate understanding of a text.
- Refer back to the text as a basis for the answers.
- Recount stories, compare and contrast, cause and effect, and sequences.
- Identify similes and metaphors in a story (the same or opposite).
- Use a variety of strategies to read words.
- Write multiple paragraphs that have beginnings, middles, and endings.
- Read more nonfiction books.

Math Goals: By the end of third grade, a child should have the following skills (but is not limited to):

- Represent and solve multiplication and division problems.
- Multiply and divide within 100.
- Read, write, and classify whole numbers and fractions.
- Explain problem solving in computation and estimation.
- Solve problems involving measurement and estimation of intervals of time, liquid volumes, and mass of objects.
- Represent and interpret data.
- Understand concepts of area and perimeter.

FOURTH GRADE

Smart Steps

- Designate time for homework and reading every day.
- Talk to your child about her day.
- Practice all basic math facts (+, -, ×, ÷).

Reading Goals: By the end of fourth grade, a child should be able to do the following (but is not limited to):

- Determine the main idea using specific details.
- Know and apply grade-level phonics and word analysis skills in decoding words.
- Read unfamiliar, multi-syllabic words in context and out of context accurately.
- Determine a theme of a story, drama, or poem from details in the text; summarize the text.
- Draw inferences and conclusions about setting, characters, and events.
- Compare and contrast narrators' different points of view.
- Write a full page or more of informational text.
- Restate the question within the answer.

Math Goals: By the end of fourth grade, a child should have the following skills (but is not limited to):

- Use the four operations (+, -, ×, ÷) with whole numbers.
- Be familiar with factors and multiples.
- Generate and analyze patterns.
- Demonstrate fluency with basic multiplication and division facts to multiples of 12.
- Understand decimals and how they relate to fractions.
- Solve problems involving measurement and conversion.
- Understand concepts of angles and measure angles.
- Draw and identify lines and angles, and classify 2D and 3D shapes by properties of their lines and angles.
- Collect data and create tables or graphs to represent it.
- Create conclusions based on data.

FIFTH GRADE

Smart Steps

- Designate time for homework and reading every night.
- Talk to your child about her school progress.
- Talk about middle school.

Reading Goals: By the end of fifth grade, a child should be able to do the following (but is not limited to):

- Read grade-level and above-grade-level text with purpose and understanding.
- Use context to confirm or self-correct word recognition and understanding, rereading as necessary.
- Quote accurately and draw inferences from a text.
- Make and confirm predictions, draw conclusions, identify cause and effect, and explain author's purpose from various genres.
- Compare and contrast two or more characters, settings, or events in a story or drama, drawing on specific details in the text (how characters interact).
- Summarize the text with details.
- Identify literal and figurative language (similes and metaphors).
- Write multiple pages of informational text.

Math Goals: By the end of fifth grade, a child should have the following skills (but is not limited to):

- Analyze patterns and relationships.
- Apply distributive and associative properties to whole numbers; draw conclusions using graphs, tables, or number sentences; and work with varying rates of change.
- Multiply and divide up to three digits.
- Use equivalent fractions as a strategy to add and subtract fractions.
- Apply and extend previous understandings of multiplication and division to multiply and divide fractions.
- Compare and order fractions and decimals to thousandths, and give equivalent forms of fractions, decimals, and percentages.
- Convert like measurement units within a given measurement system.
- Geometric measurement: understand concepts of volume and relate volume to multiplication and to addition.
- Solve problems using elapsed time.
- Graph points on a grid to solve real-world and mathematical problems.

There it is—kindergarten to fifth grade outlined by reading and math goals. Students should know (but are not limited to) each of these skills to be considered advanced and on the right path to:

- Algebra I by grade 8 (with a C or higher)
- Algebra II by grade 11 (with a C or higher)
- 3 or better on the AP Exam, 4 on the IB Exam
- 24 on the ACT, 1650 on the SAT

These lists of reading and math goals may seem tedious and specific, but they are proven Common Core skills that lead to advanced knowledge and advanced foundations for future learning to take place. And while they may seem overly detailed, it's because students and parents need to know how to play the game if they are going to win. Just like in sports, deep practice produces automatic skills. The more students and their parents, along with schools, ingrain deep practice of key skills into their brains and actions, the more mastery of the skills happens.

In middle school and high school, students begin to take more responsibility for their own education. Students can be selective in courses and extracurricular activities. However, parental support at this level is still important. Schools and parents should begin to talk about college if that hasn't already been discussed before. Let students know that the future is college. Don't make college a choice. Make college the goal.

At the middle school level, start talking about Lexiles. A Lexile is a nationally normed score that categorizes how well a student is reading and understanding. A Lexile score ranges from 200 for early reading books to 1600 for more advanced texts. The higher the Lexile level, the greater the difficulty of texts. For example, *Don Quixote* by Cervantes is leveled at 1500, and the US Constitution is 1560. *Pride and Prejudice* by Jane Austen is leveled at 1100, as is *Vincent Van Gogh: Portrait of an Artist* by Jan Greenberg and Sandra Jordan. By comparison, US newspapers tend to have a Lexile reading level of between fifth and ninth grade, or 800–1000.

Students should fall into the following Lexile levels in middle school:

Sixth grade: 1050+
Seventh grade: 1110+
Eighth grade: 1150+

The reading Lexiles are a good indicator of comprehension and reading skill. They measure how well a student reads a certain difficulty of material. The challenge is to engage students at high levels of texts. That challenge pushes and stretches students' capacity to increase their vocabulary and fluency. Even in middle school, just like for early learners, it's all about literacy.

Also in middle school, students and parents should think about what a well-rounded education looks like. Not only do students need a strong reading capacity, but they also need strong math skills. In math, students who are college-bound typically have the following courses:

Sixth grade: general math
Seventh grade: pre-algebra
Eighth grade: Algebra I

College-bound and advanced students also have science, geography, history, government, foreign language, physical education/health, art, music, and technology in middle school. In addition, this is when participation in extracurricular activities such as athletics, clubs, and mentoring become important to forming a well-rounded educational experience. Don't overschedule your child with extracurricular activities, but let your student be involved in what interests him. This is the time to explore the paths that will eventually lead to college-level choices of majors and a career.

High school is a continuation of everything that a child has learned to that point in her formal educational experience. High school fine-tunes the skills necessary for college when students take the right courses. *Right courses* means advanced placement, honors, and dual-credit courses. Even if it is a stretch for a student to take higher-level courses, that should be the choice. These courses reflect the rigor that is required for college success. Push students to explore the rigorous courses.

Here is a quick outline of what an advanced high school student's schedule over four years might look like:

Math—Four years: Mathematics coursework emphasizes college-preparatory algebra and other content of comparable or greater rigor. Students who complete algebra in eighth grade might take geometry, trigonometry, algebra II, and then advanced placement calculus.

Science—Four years: Science coursework emphasizes college-preparatory biology and chemistry. Coursework should include at least one laboratory course.

Communication arts—Four years: English and language arts coursework emphasizes college-preparatory composition, research skills, and analysis of literature. Speech and debate courses may also be included.

Social studies—Three to four years: Social studies coursework emphasizes American history, government, state history, geography, and global studies.

Foreign language—Two to four years: Coursework in foreign language emphasizes written and spoken language skills in languages such as French, Spanish, Latin, and German.

Fine Arts—One semester to four years: Fine arts coursework emphasizes visual arts, instrumental or vocal music, dance, and theater. Theory or appreciation courses may also be offered.

While these specific categories outline the necessary courses required for a college-preparatory mindset, there are other things that students and parents need to consider while a student is in high school. For example, students should take the ACT—a national college admissions exam that tests a student's skills in communication arts, math, reading, and science. This test should be taken, at the very latest, during a student's junior year. The ACT score goal should be a 24+. This score is a good indicator of future college success.

Just like in middle school, high school students should have a well-rounded experience. By being involved in extracurricular activities, leadership positions, mentoring, and volunteering roles, students get to see a *bigger picture* of the world around them. Colleges and universities like to see high academic marks, but they also want the students who enjoyed a wide array of high school activities and leadership roles.

This course of study sounds glamorous and rigorous. It is. But it's not meant to be so rigorous and glamorous that it's unreachable for the chunk of students who typically land in the middle of the pack. It's the *middle of the pack* students who need the extra challenge to reach the higher level of rigor. This is where support systems of tutoring, ACT preparatory classes, and extended time for activities like robotics and debate team come into play. Extra support for all students creates safety nets that allow students to work at a pace and level always within reach. There can be no excuse of insufficient access to extra help and support. Schools should commit to that notion just as much as parents should.

Schools can be creative when it comes to carving out time for the extra support that kids need. Maybe it's holding a tutoring café, where students can go during lunch to work on specific projects or papers. Maybe it's before school when the math teachers all come in early to work on problems, data, and make-up tests. The point is that there is only so much classroom time during the day. Schools, students, and parents should have the flexibility and creativity to make time for the important extra work that goes into supporting kids at high levels. Schools have to be accommodating. Parents have to be accommodating. Working together, with flexibility, commitment, and specific goals, schools and parents can help students achieve at higher levels.

The span of time from infancy to high school is a parent's time to watch her child grow and learn—not only learning the social and emotional part of love, nurturing, support, laughter, challenge, success, and failure, but also learning the academic ropes. Learning the ingredients of literacy, vocabulary, writing, math, and science prepares children for a lifetime of tools to navigate this big world.

It is such a short time that parents have their kids at home before the kids leave their nest. Shouldn't that short time be devoted to providing the things critically necessary for being successful in life? By providing literacy, love, nurturing, support, and encouragement, parents are providing the best start for their child's life. Kids learn from their parents. Parents have to use this short time be a teacher, model, and unrelenting example of hard work and grit.

It doesn't mean all work and no play. It means always thinking about raising children with literacy, communication, and urgency in mind, and it's good to have fun along the way. Being a parent is a parent's most important job. As a job, there are certain things that a parent is going to be evaluated on. Most parents are devastated by a marked-down evaluation at work. Shouldn't they feel even more so when it's a mark against their job as a parent? Why should parents get a pass when it comes to raising successful children?

They shouldn't. And that's why schools and other parents are here to help. Teaching the fundamental academic skills from infancy to high school can be done. Use the guidelines in this chapter to do so, and to help schools and parents know what needs to be taught and learned.

Academics are the standard of comparison to which all other parts of a school have to measure up. Being smart is the way out. Being smart is the ticket to college and career. When it's the norm for students to be smart and academically focused, the school and the parents have succeeded. But even after creating a culture in which the norm is to have successful students who are achieving at high levels, the work does not end. It's an ever-evolving process to grow and learn.

The guidelines in this chapter, however, fundamentally don't change. The importance of literacy at the earliest start of life, the importance of reading and writing and communicating, the importance of math, the importance of exploring different interests, the importance of rigorous courses, and the importance of a laser-like focus on parents doing what's best for kids—all of these will never change. While this is not a *parenting* book, it is certainly a book about the things parents can do to raise high-achieving kids. It's the steps outlined in this chapter that will contribute to parents being informed about the parts of their child's education that they can influence.

It's all about academics. Giving the gift of literacy and academic toughness is one of the best gifts a parent will give her child. It's also the best gift a school will give its students.

Chapter summary: The rules in this chapter are the essential items that parents and schools need to follow to make kids advanced and ready for college. The expectations are high, but what else should we expect from our students? When parents don't know what the rules are, they can't follow them. When schools don't know what the rules are, they can't follow them. Please follow these guidelines when raising babies and students. These guidelines level the playing field for all kids when followed and nurtured.

EIGHT
Inclusion

In order to have academic credibility and students achieving at a high level, not only do the guidelines outlined in the previous chapter have to be followed, but there also has to be a sense of inclusion of all students. The belief that only a handful of students (the bell curve) will rise to the top has to be challenged. All students have to be given the exposure to rigorous academics, and all students, no matter where they live in this country, are part of your school in some way.

Students today are more mobile than ever. Schools see transfers between surrounding school districts in large metropolitan areas on a regular basis. Schools can almost predict certain times of the year when there might be an influx of transfers based on several factors. Maybe an apartment complex changed payment policies. Maybe parents moved because they wanted a better school for their child. Maybe boundary lines shifted. Whatever the cause, it's no secret that mobility among high-poverty populations is rampant.

Because of the high mobility rate, schools have to be prepared to accept all students. Think about the story of the seed kernel and the pollen. There is a seed kernel that grows and produces pollen that floats in the air. The pollen's fate of where it lands and grows depends on where the wind blows it. Now, the farmer wants only the best seed kernels and pollen on his property, but he cannot control what blows in from the north, east, west, or south. He can only control what's on his own property. So isn't it in the farmer's best interest to help ensure that all the seed kernels and pollen on all the surrounding properties are also the best? If the farmer helps all the surrounding farmers produce high-quality seed, then there is an exponentially higher rate of success for the pollen that gets swept up and blown away.

All students, like all seed, affect all schools. Students will float through schools. Parents will float through schools. But the common factor remains: the schools. All students are part of all schools in some little way.

Think about the global statistics of reading and math (and not just the neighboring school district's statistics). Of the thirty-four economically developed countries (as categorized by the Organization for Economic Cooperation and Development), the United States falls in the middle of the pack for reading literacy when measuring the reading levels of fifteen-year-olds. There are approximately six countries that outscore the United States, sixteen countries that score below the United States, and about fourteen countries score about the same as the United States.[1]

In math, of the forty-seven countries participating in *The Trends in International Mathematics and Science Study* (TIMSS), US eighth graders' average mathematics score was higher than the average scores of thirty-seven other countries, lower than the scores of five countries, and not measurably different from five other countries. All of the education systems that outperformed the United States in math were in Asia—Chinese Taipei, Hong Kong, Japan, the Republic of South Korea, and Singapore.[2]

With as much innovation and opportunity that this country provides, there is no reason that the United States shouldn't score higher in reading literacy and math.

Most educators have heard the data about US reading scores and math scores compared to other countries. Sometimes educators wonder if parents care about this data. The history of this country shows an overwhelmingly competitive nature among our citizens, but are we competitive enough when it comes to education?

To reach the level of reading literacy and math competency that is needed to be considered at the top among our global counterparts, parents and educators both have to start being tougher and smarter to forge ahead in the competition. The US population is becoming more urban. Cities are growing at rates far faster than rural areas. With this realization, urban core schools have to pick up the pace in order to compete in the national (and global) arena.

The global statistics and the lag in US performance is a catalyst for some people to spark change. But taking this global and national information and comparing it to your local schools will influence the most change. The not-in-my-backyard mentality has to kick in. The outrage that failing education systems should incite is just not present. Why? Only when schools throughout the United States recognize that, as a collaborative whole, they are going to fail or succeed together, will schools start to change. All schools have to care about the success of all schools.

When the academic rigor of schools is lifted to reflect the real talent and capability of its students, the theme of inclusion has to then start to be solidified in schools. Schools have to create a welcoming environment for all students, parents, and staff. The environment should feel like everyone is welcome and valued. The tough kids, the tough parents, the tough staff members—all of these people have to feel that the school cares about them being a part of the whole. The schools have to teach students and parents (and even school staff members) how to be a part of an open, engaging, and welcoming community.

Ask for input from parents and students—not on all ideas and initiatives, but on some. Keep the office doors open, the principal's office door open, and invite people in. Build a school that is the hub of activity and learning for the community.

A welcoming environment also includes working with other organizations in the community. Make it easy to work with your schools, and only work with reputable businesses, services, charities, and people. Schools and parents have to have support from outside entities for social services. Social services like food banks, shelters, churches, volunteer organizations, antiviolence organizations, and community centers have to be partners with schools. This partnership is based on trust, shared mission and goals, and reputation. Schools and parents need help, but it has to be help that has been vetted and proven to help kids.

When schools and parents have the support from outside services, hungry kids, abused kids, and poor kids have opportunities to pull from multiple resources. Schools and parents have to give the best opportunities for children. When parents can't do it alone or can't access resources on their own, schools should help. School social workers are miracle workers. School social workers provide the link between learning and meeting basic needs. Clothes, food, shelter, furniture, a ride home, groceries—these are things that kids need before they can be ready to learn.

In thinking about groceries, schools should participate in weekend and summer backpack snack programs. This is when local churches, food banks, or food pantries load up backpacks for certain students to take home over the weekend to provide food for the kids if it's not readily available in their homes. Hunger is a real issue in urban schools. We have to feed kids and they need to know that a stable source of nutrition is coming home each weekend, because the care that schools provide doesn't end on Friday afternoons.

An established system of providing these basic needs has to be in place to ensure kids and parents have them if the parents can't provide it on their own. By enlisting the help of the community and the community's reputable social service providers, schools can boost the offerings beyond academics. This creates a safe, welcoming hub. Schools should be that place.

Schools should be the welcoming places that believe that all students are their students. By focusing on each student in its classroom but also being aware of all the other kids out there, schools create a sense of inclusion in their mission. While it's about each individual student, it's also about all students and where schools want all students to be in the future. Pushing a mass of students in the same direction starts with one student, and each student has a valuable contribution to your schools.

Each student has a valuable contribution to a school and each student's parents are part of that connection. When students and their parents feel welcome and included in their school, they feel connected. Trusted relationships are built from connections. Schools are then free to push the envelope on academics and expectations when those connections are strong. Welcome all students with care and deliberate inclusion. Schools should do the same with parents. Envelop students and parents with the sense that everyone belongs and everyone achieves.

Chapter summary: All students and their parents belong to all schools. Every child shares a common title with all other kids in this country: student. When schools can understand that it takes all of us to share the responsibility to educate every student, then schools can learn how to do so in better ways. Parents need to understand this sense of inclusion too. Parents can help other parents be better. The really good moms and dads want to make sure all kids feel a sense of belonging and connection to school because the really good moms and dads understand that other kids are going to affect their own child. Let's help everyone be better. Let's connect everyone to the school experience.

NOTES

1. "U.S. Department of Education, National Center for Education Statistics," http://nces.ed.gov/ (August 2013).
2. Ibid.

NINE
Keeping Tension on the System

When everyone belongs and feels connected to the school experience, a sense of comfort can spread throughout schools. That comfort is good. Very good. But it can also be crippling if left to run amok. Comfort, or contentment, can breed complacency.

Schools have to keep tension on the system. Schools have to keep tension on the staff, students, and parents, and vice versa. Think about a rubber band. When you try to shoot a rubber band and it doesn't get stretched enough, it droops. If it gets stretched too far, it breaks. There is a point of tension that is just right when pulling on a rubber band. The right tension is somewhere in the middle of not pulling enough and pulling too hard. Schools have to find the right balance of pushing just hard enough so that the staff and students don't break, yet at the same time ensuring that they are constantly working hard and smart.

To keep improving, schools have to push the limits on comfort and complacency. Keeping tension on the system is about knowing your roots and knowing the skills outlined in chapter 7, while always thinking about the next steps to higher achievement. Pushing the limits on staff, students, and parents is delicate business, but it's a necessary one.

Something to consider when thinking about keeping tension on the system and continually getting better, is involving everyone in the conversation. Instill the notion of having to evolve to get better among the staff, internally, and then think about how it will look from the outside (parents and community).

Begin the conversation of next steps as an internal conversation in the schools—leaders, the board of education, teachers—and natural themes will develop from those conversations. After establishing the standards of learning outlined in chapter 7, talk about the vision going forward. The vision for the future should still revolve around academics and raising the achievement level of all kids. It should still involve the goal of being a high-performing school district—a consistently high-performing school district.

To do this, schools need to keep thinking about how to involve parents more in the process of learning. While this book has outlined the steps students and parents need to learn to be advanced, there has to also be a way to communicate the steps to parents. Are some parents going to read this book? Yes. But it's the parents who will not read this book with whom the schools need to work most.

How do schools reach out and involve parents in the process? The idea is that the information about the important milestones and about the skills that all kids need to succeed is communicated in an effective and meaningful way, in a collective way that ensures all parents (and schools) are on the same page.

Schools should create some content around the Common Core State Standards and make that content available in the schools. To ensure that the communication is meaningful and lasting, make the content resonate internally with staff first. Then push the content out to parents and the community.

When thinking about a plan of action that tackles the issue of college readiness and how to push the information out to the parents, schools have to consider the entire scope of kids—from birth to grade 12. Focus on the babies first, as was presented in chapter 7.

Each district should have an early childhood team. This team might consist of a Parents As Teachers (PAT) director, an early childhood center principal or director, and elementary principals. The first task is to figure out how to communicate the importance of literacy and provide direction on being kindergarten-ready in your school district. Use the guidelines outlined in this book for the content, and then think about how that gets translated to the parents.

Think about what young families with babies and toddlers use throughout the course of their days. What is the best medium to convey the message you want them to hear and see? Is it a poster on the wall above the changing table in the baby's room or a magnet on the refrigerator for the mom to see during the twenty-plus times she opens the refrigerator door throughout the day? This medium will be virtually the same for all families with babies and toddlers.

This message cannot stress enough the importance of parents reading everyday with their child, of talking with their child, of playing with their child—the vocabulary piece and the positive interaction piece. This exercise will help schools again learn how to help parents understand what it takes to *raise* a child. This means the project demands a shift in focus from merely teaching kids and caring about the school environment to focusing on all families and kids not only at school but also at home.

Think about what moms and dads with young children do throughout the day. The sleep-deprived, ever-moving blur of parenthood can wear on young parents. As educators, take time to consider what these family's lives are like. How can schools help these parents teach their kids literacy and communication? Use this thought process when creating a plan of communication for them.

After meeting with the early childhood team, meet with the next levels. Meet with the elementary team, then the middle school team, and finally the high school team. With collaboration at each level, meet with teachers, support staff, counselors, and principals to compile your essential steps from birth through grade 12 (hint: use the guidelines in chapter 7 as the steps).

Once the school has an outline of essential components and messages, go to the board of education to present the work to that point. Have a conversation with the board of education about what the project should look like. Ask for input. Know that the project and action plan should look professional—it should be an example of which students and families can be proud. It should be an extension of the work the schools have already done to be achieving at higher levels.

After bringing the board of education into the confidences of the project, the design and feel of the project should come next. Is the design and medium used to convey the plan something that the school district can produce on its own? If the school district is large, it might have a printing and design team. Use the resources your schools have available and work within those capabilities.

Or perhaps it might be a project that needs to enlist the help of a professional design firm or outside resources to pull it all together. Professional design firms have the expertise to provide cross-sectional advice. Outsiders tend to have all kinds of advice on how to run a school district. Good or bad, this means that professional design firms and professionals who don't work in schools have people who see into a school district differently from those within it.

The people who work on projects that reach into family homes need to produce a story that will come to life with the school district's families. Whoever is working on this project needs to remember that it's not just words and sentences thrown together on a piece of paper that is getting distributed to parents and kids. They need to remember that it's a story about all kids and the importance of what they do every day that matters. They also need to remember that they are representing a brand and what that brand means to parents and kids.

Check out design firms in the local area. Think about firms that know the community and who want to be involved in projects with kids. Also think about firms that have experience with all kinds of business sectors throughout the country. This provides an extra area of expertise, and the outside insight can help ensure that the project will resonate with any child and family in the nation and not just in your local community. You want a project that stands the test of the nation's children, a project that is applicable to any child, whether they live in Kansas City or in New York City.

Talk to friends and colleagues who have worked with design firms before. Word of mouth is an excellent way to find the right fit for a design relationship. Most business happens through references anyway. This goes back to quality people. Make sure your schools employ the best people so that they can in turn collaborate with only the best professionals who work outside the district.

If the school decides to work with an outside firm to help with the project, talk to the design team about the elements that make the school special and unique and what the project means for educating any student in any school. The project should have universal appeal, but it should have district-specific assessment scores and benchmarks that are applicable to your schools highlighted throughout the project.

Working with schools might be uncharted territory for some professional design firms. Their client lists might include large, well-known clients like architecture firms, clothing stores, and upscale eateries. But not schools. That is what schools should like about an outside design firm though—a point of view outside the education sector.

Looking into a school district from the private sector, schools might look like a conglomeration of apples and school bus stationary with stick figures writing on a chalkboard. This is no longer a relevant snapshot of what schools do today. To be relevant, schools and their designs and messages have to connect with what kids (and parents) see in the current culture of technology, cartoons, television, and the Internet. Schools should want what the big brands have.

Of course, school district budgets are mostly limited, so start with what makes sense financially and work within those boundaries. A good and reputable design firm will work with school districts simply because of the nature of the nonprofit business.

Talk about several concepts with the design team. In each concept, remember that it is important to have a central theme as the overarching idea. Talk to the design firm in the initial meetings about what your schools are like. Talk about the students and teachers, the parents, and the community around your schools. Then help translate this demographic-type information into goals for your schools. The focus for most schools should revolve around the idea of being advanced, focusing on reading and math, and providing a pathway to college.

When the design team, whether an outside firm or internal team, presents the concepts for the project, ask some students to join the presentation. These students should be from all levels of the district—from elementary to high school. The students are the voices that the design team will hear the loudest because the students tend to be the most concise when voicing what they want.

Listen to how the students talk about the concepts. Listen to the excitement or disappointment in the student's reaction to the concepts. Once the presentation is complete, have all the students leave the room. Then, individually, ask each one back into the room. Ask each student for his thoughts on the concepts, what he likes and doesn't like, and what seems relevant to his life.

There might not be unanimous sentiment for one concept, but there should be an overwhelming sense of one concept's likability among the students. Make a decision about the concept based on the students' input, but also choose the concept that speaks to the school's team. Further vet the concept with select parents and administrators. This could include hosting mini focus groups of parents and teachers, or it could include taking some parents out to lunch and showing them the project to solicit some informal observations. The point is to just generally get a feel for how accepted it would be among a small, select group.

Once the concept is chosen, commit to it wholeheartedly. Begin to think about all the offshoots that can come from the single concept. From the medium that a school district will actually hand out to its parents, students, teachers, and community to the banners that might hang on the school walls, think about all the ways the concept can be realized within your schools and your community.

The project used to convey the school's content and message of college readiness will be an extension of the schools and it will help students and parents be aware of what it takes to make it from birth to grade twelve, ready for college. A project of this magnitude should organically amplify what a school already does in its day-to-day operations. Name the project something simple and straightforward. The beauty of a project starts in the name. For example, if the name of the project is Made Smart, most students and parents will know what the project aims to do. Kids are *made smart* by what they and their parents do. The schools are here to help them.

After the name or theme of the project is decided upon, think about what materials will be used to distribute the project. Maybe it's educational booklets with *Smart Steps* (hint: use the *smart steps* in chapter 7) and bullet point lists of reading goals and math goals. Have the booklets focus on the overarching themes of reading and math. Literacy and math have to be the key starting points in helping students and parents know what is expected in high-achieving, college-preparatory schools.

The educational booklets will be the guidelines wrapped in a neat package. This is like a handy reference guide to quickly look up, by age and grade, what a student should be doing at a particular level in order to be advanced.

In the birth–pre-kindergarten booklet, the focus should be on things like reading bedtime stories, pretending, making up songs, and putting on performances. Remember what is fun and inherent and innocent in being a child and put those things in the birth–pre-kindergarten guidelines. Remember snuggling in before bedtime and picking out a favorite book, and translate that into the instructional guide. Remember making up stories and songs, and put it in the instructional guide. Remember pretend play with made-up toys and acting out performances on a stage made of cardboard boxes, and put that in an instructional guide. The key is to make the project reflect what childhood is about in the early learning guide.

In association with the content, be deliberate about the pictures and graphics used to convey the feeling of childhood and high expectations. Create pictures and graphics that incorporate a true feeling of whimsy and functionality. How the graphics illustrate the content should not be coincidental . Students and parents want fun in their lives along with the everyday content. Have fun with the graphics. Again, make it relevant to what students and parents see in the barrage of media flashing across their phones and computer screens each day. Make it current, but don't make it phony or inauthentic. Kids and parents can see right through phoniness.

For the elementary portion of the guidelines or instructions, continue the theme and concept, but think about a differentiating graphic or illustration. There should be a way for students and parents to differentiate the levels of school by looking at the guides.

If your school chooses the educational booklet route, continue the Smart Steps section and maybe separate the pages by grade level. Make each grade level have a page of reading and math goals aligned with the Common Core State Standards (see chapter 7) and with what is important for advanced students to know.

Keep in mind what might be important for one school might differ slightly for another school. Make sure to continue the flair or spirit of your schools in each piece. Meaning, if drama is popular at your school, highlight some drama pages. If reading nonfiction books is big at your school, highlight more nonfiction reading instructions.

Make sure each grade level page also states the reading level/book level to achieve. This reading level and book level will align with each school's own assessments and practice tests. For example, does your district use the Developmental Reading Assessment (DRA), Lexiles, or Scholastic Reading Inventory (SRI)?

Take whatever assessment pieces your district uses and put those goals in the guidelines. Then put a glossary in the back of the guide so that parents (and teachers) can understand what the terms mean. This is also a natural conversation during parent/teacher conferences. Have your teachers pull out the guidebooks and show the students and parents where the student lands on the assessment index. This allows parents to closely monitor the assessments and actually know what they mean. This helps the parent and the teacher. It's a natural rubric.

The secondary educational booklet, or whatever form your project has taken, should contain the middle school and high school guidelines for creating advanced students. This booklet will probably look a bit different because these students will start to create an individualized path. But reinforce the fact that there are particular requirements that certainly produce college-and-career-ready students. For example, are you instructing students (and their parents) to take advanced placement (AP) courses, a foreign language, or the ACT or SAT?

The guidelines in the middle school and high school part of the action plan should start to hone in on college choice and preparation. While all of the steps leading up to the middle school and high school portion are equally important as the foundation of a college-ready student, the secondary guide should talk about specific goals for college entrance.

It starts with talking about college and available resources. It also starts with reading at advanced levels in middle school. Also, algebra at the eighth-grade level with a C or better has been proven as an indicator of college success. (Use the guidelines outlined in chapter 7 as the criteria for creating your content.)

As described in chapter 7, the steps for the middle school and high school students and parents should also account for the ACT or SAT college admittance tests. Encourage all juniors in the school district's high schools to take the appropriate test. Describe the tests in the guide—talk about what the test is like and why it's important. It might also be helpful to again provide a glossary of terms in the back of the guidelines.

After the booklets, guides, or whatever medium the schools chose to implement are completed, create additional materials that can be associated with the initiative. This includes trying to figure out what students and staff would actually use and/or wear. Whatever is produced, it's important that each student and staff get one.

Is it a magnet that is broken down into birth to pre-kindergarten, elementary school, middle school, and high school pieces? Maybe these four magnets join to make a poster that looks like a map from birth through grade 12? Give each student and parent a magnet (according to their age or grade) and a poster along with their respective educational booklet. These can be distributed at your back-to-school enrollment festivities. What a positive and energetic way to start a school year!

Schools should obviously want each student to feel connected to the action plan and most students feel like their clothing represents how they feel and who they are. Think about each student getting a project T-shirt. The school's staff should also receive a T-shirt. Then think about coordinated days when the students and staff wear the shirts together.

And wouldn't it be great to have a T-shirt that can be worn to all district events in which students are performing or gathering? This T-shirt can automatically join an entire student body in solidarity with the college-ready message blazing across the front or back. Wouldn't it also be rewarding to see the students wear the shirts on the weekends at the community centers and at the shopping centers? How will you know if you chose the right design for your students? If they wear the shirt in public!

Produce some stickers with the design on them as well. What a great reminder to students about their progress in being college-ready when a teacher can pat them on the back and put a sticker on their shirt announcing their compliance with the guidelines. Order by the ten thousands and make the stickers available to the principals and teachers.

Button pins are also a popular item for students to collect on their backpacks. Make several designs from the initiative and slap the designs on button pins. Hand the buttons out to students at school events and in school. The more associations provided to students and parents that reinforce the message of college readiness, the better chance they have of identifying with the concept and working on the goals that have been set.

Don't forget the teachers and staff. Teachers love gifts—especially when they are usable and relevant to what they do every day in the classroom. Do your teachers use coffee mugs, SMARTBoards, or iPad covers? Design items with what teachers use in mind and include the college readiness initiative message on the items.

When thinking about extra materials that enhance the college readiness message, it's productive to think about *the hook*—that quick depiction of a graphic or a recurring tone in each piece of the overall concept. Maybe it's an attribute or characteristics in addition to the content that is important for student success. Use the characteristics that kids need for success on the back of each educational booklet and on the T-shirts. Have the characteristics highlight the components that are important for students and parents to purposefully grasp—things like perseverance, hard work, parent support, grit, study time, love, and collaboration.

The reference to characteristics of success should illustrate the non-quantitative qualities that should be part of students' lives. For example, the early childhood piece can highlight bedtime stories, play time, song singing, paper and crayons, and pure nurturing.

The elementary piece can instruct hard work, participation, enthusiasm, cooperation, and asking questions.

The secondary piece can conclude with study time, hard work, participation, ambition, and parental support. These are the essence of a well-rounded education and, when combined with proven academic benchmarks, these qualities can produce high-performing students. Make it about academics and character traits.

What will these attributes look like in your schools? Have the administrative team brainstorm about their top qualities in students and parents and then include those qualities in the college readiness materials. This shows that the school's focus is more than pounding out high rigor and expectations, indicating a softer side of understanding the emotional part of things that aren't necessarily teachable. Always remember to think about the *bigger picture*. It's not just about academics—it's also about creating healthy, loving, nurtured, hard-working students.

Then use all the extra items created to coordinate school days to show off the initiative. Have a day in which all the students and teachers wear their T-shirts and call it the [insert theme] day. Invite local media outlets to cover the day and highlight the content of the college readiness message while providing that beautiful visual of your design.

The publicity generated by the college readiness project is publicity that can't be bought. The project also meets the criteria of reporting on academically oriented stories only because the context of the story ends up being about the college readiness initiative and how the schools are implementing high standards for advanced students. See how that works?

After rolling out the content-rich guides to the students and parents, and after talking to the students and parents about the content, take some time to reflect on the process. Begin to talk to the local community about the project. Spread the college readiness message into the business community, church community, local chambers of commerce, whatever fits the community's vibe.

Know that the spin-offs of button pins, T-shirts, bookmarks, stickers, coffee mugs, or whatever is used to show the message, are used not only as marketing materials to bolster your school's image but also to remind students and parents that every day is a college readiness day. Remember, too, that it's not just about trinkets and giveaways. It's also about the spirit and the message of what your students hear each and every day. It's the intent and the goal that these reminders help students understand that college readiness is a journey and adventure that has to be nurtured and cultivated. It doesn't happen overnight.

These reminders should seep into the community too. The community has to be the next line of support for students and parents. Is the local corporate community aware of the work your students, parents, and schools are doing? Are the local doctor and dentist aware of your parents' struggles? Do your engineering firms, architecture firms, design firms, accounting firms, and law firms know that students have an action plan for college readiness and that they are being prepared as the future workforce?

This is how to keep tension on the system. These types of initiatives push students and parents and the community to think about education differently. It pushes them to think about education as a series of steps that are essential to being college ready. Schools, parents, and students cannot slack. The tension, the ongoing quest for greatness, cannot be by chance. It has to be deliberate. The drive and rigor that schools intentionally crank out will translate to their students and parents. Find the balance of rigor and intensity and lay it out, step by step, for parents and students.

Schools should always be about the next level. They should be about mastering one level and moving on to the next highest at all times. Keep getting better. Keep pushing. But don't forget to bring the parents and students along too.

Chapter summary: There are things that schools can do to show parents the way to raise successful students. Parents have to help in order for schools to be high performing. Schools, especially schools of poverty and low achievement, have to have parent help if they are going to make it. Parents can no longer use the excuses that *they don't know what to do* or *I'm not going to do that*. When schools enlist the help of parents, schools can begin to harness the full effect of all adults tag teaming together to raise students up to the levels they are capable of. Keep tension on the system. Show parents what their jobs are and hold them accountable.

TEN
The Heart of a School

Sometimes educators can forget about the little things in life. Sometimes educators focus on all the high-level educational jargon and the next big curriculum initiative that they forget about investing in the process of bringing students and parents along for the ride. At the heart of schools is the heart of the people—kids, teachers, leaders, and parents. Every day, schools are working with the most important asset for our future: the kids.

The question is this: Is it right for what we want our kids to look like in the future? Surely life has always seemed fast paced, especially to parents who watch their children grow up so quickly. But the time now seems to go faster and change quicker than ever before. Technology, the workforce, new ways of thinking—all of these big ideas shift faster than ever. The immediacy of social media, the twenty-four-hour news cycle, and global access connects everyone all the time. Saying this, with all the connections and communication and immediacy, we still don't know what the future will look like. Can it really get faster and better and more accessible? Sure.

But the question still remains in all the whirl of life and connection: What will our kids look like in the future? And what can we do to ensure that children continue to be nurtured, loved, and smart in the midst of all the noise around them?

The characteristics of what being a kid is all about will hopefully never change. Childhood means playing, reading, pretending, running, digging in the dirt, exploring, listening, talking, laughing, being silly, and being nurtured. Childhood is the only time in a child's life in which he will emotionally and physically need to be nurtured and connected with in a very specific way for him to be ready to accept and face the world's ways.

Research shows that kids who are not nurtured, don't receive instant response to crying in infancy, aren't cuddled, don't receive eye contact, and don't receive the bond of another human can't make the neurological connections necessary for proper development. Until the child experiences the solid bond of love, nurturing, communication, response, connection, and safety, he will have a difficult time being able to recoup the emotional capacity to learn and succeed later in life. Childhood is the only chance parents have to get it right. Parents and children can't go back. They can only go forward.

If schools and parents want to prepare students for the future, then they have to start looking at education slightly differently. Schools have to start thinking about what it takes to raise kids outside of the school setting. Parents have to start thinking more about what it really takes to help schools before their children even reach school age. The days of *it's the school's responsibility* or *it's the parent's responsibility* are over. Education is everyone's responsibility. The two should be so intertwined that they may be indistinguishable.

Think about it. Don't the best teachers act like the best parents? And don't the best parents act like the best teachers? The two are linked.

It's time to get real about schools and parents working together. While the two entities are surely linked, they each have their own individual responsibilities at the same time. Meaning, while a teacher or principal might act as a mom to a child, there is still a mom at home waiting for her daughter to come home from school for dinner and bedtime. And while a mom is working her day job, there is a teacher at school teaching children the things that will help build space stations on the moon. Children need both parents and teachers. They need the love, support, encouragement, and push that parents and teachers together provide.

It's the parents' fault that kids are failing these days. What about that statement is true? Many times a student's failure is influenced by her parents' ability. Some parents just don't get it or don't care, and if this is true, then isn't it about time we start doing something to help parents? It's time to bring the parents into the confidences of how to raise successful kids and students. It shouldn't be a secret that only the privileged know.

Is there anyone better to share the secret and help the parents than the schools? Schools may complain about the parents, but complaining doesn't help anyone. Face the problem head on, and figure out a way to show parents what's right. If schools don't want it to get worse, then they have to figure out how to make it better.

The fragility of following guidelines and doing the right things necessary for college readiness rely on the contributions of both parents and schools. Beautiful things are strong yet fragile. Beautiful schools full of achieving students are strong and yet so fragile. The energy, deep passion, and unrelenting willingness to not fail on behalf of one another should be ingrained in both parents and schools. Make a beautiful system that requires everyone's contribution.

This connection between parents and schools does not have to be solely codependent, though. Schools have their own expertise in areas and so do parents. Schools can get out in front of the parents on some issues, and parents can get out in front of schools on some issues. But the common respect and appreciation for both points of view have to remain the focus. Parents and schools have to remember to connect with students at the students' level. Whether schools are pushing for higher goals or the parents are pushing for more programs, each has to remember to connect with students.

Connecting means remembering what childhood is like. Remember the things in your own childhood that truly meant what it was to be valued. It wasn't the book, but it was the time spent reading. It wasn't the weather, but it was the adventure hiking in the woods. It wasn't the peanut butter and jelly sandwich, but it was the picnic on the family room floor together. It wasn't the words, but it was the story. It wasn't the cardboard cutout frame, but it was the impromptu puppet show in the hallway. And it wasn't the color of the crayon, but it was the picture on the paper.

All of the things in childhood don't have to revolve around *academics*, but in the end, the activities and interests of students do get shaped by *learning*. Schools and parents have to focus on the process of *learning*—learning about responsibility, about people, about messages, about accountability, about relationships, about literacy and math, about inclusion, and about perseverance in spite of failure.

Parents and schools need to keep thinking about the reality of kids today. A child's future is mostly determined by parents and schools. Parents and schools have to have the same standards for their students. Even though students may come from backgrounds of poverty or abuse or parents who don't have a high school diploma, it doesn't mean that they are exempt from getting an advanced education. Parents and schools together have to make the leap to change perceptions of what it really is that happens in schools.

Schools are moms and dads, helpers and supporters, nurturers and guides, and teachers and leaders. At the same time, parents are moms and dads, helpers and supporters, nurturers and guides, and teachers and leaders. And because parents and schools are all of those things, shouldn't we be working together to raise successful children?

It's on you, parents and schools. Get to work.

References

Hart, Betty, and Todd R. Risley. *Meaningful Differences in the Everyday Experience of Young American Children*. Baltimore: Paul H. Brookes, 1995.

———. "Meaningful Differences in the Everyday Experience of Young American Children." strategiesforchildren.org. August 2013. http://www.strategiesforchildren.org/eea/6research_summaries/05_MeaningfulDifferences.pdf.

"National Center for Children in Poverty." nccp.org. August 2013. http://www.nccp.org/tools/risk/ (accessed August 15, 2013).

"U.S. Department of Education, National Center for Education Statistics." http://nces.ed.gov/. August 2013. http://nces.ed.gov/fastfacts/display.asp?id=1 (accessed August 15, 2013).

"The United States of Education: The Changing Demographics of the United States and Their Schools." centerforpubliceducation.org. August 2013. http://www.centerforpubliceducation.org/You-May-Also-Be-Interested-In-landing-page-level/Organizing-a-School-YMABI/The-United-States-of-education-The-changing-demographics-of-the-United-States-and-their-schools.html (accessed August 15, 2013).